Standard Written English

Standard Written English
A Guide

Philip Gaskell

Edinburgh University Press

© Philip Gaskell, 1998

Edinburgh University Press
22 George Square, Edinburgh

Typeset in Sabon
by Norman Tilley Graphics, Northampton,
and printed and bound in Great Britain
by The University Press, Cambridge

A CIP record for this book is available from
the British Library

ISBN 0 7486 1135 5 (hardback)
ISBN 0 7486 1136 3 (paperback)

Dedicated to
Tilda
with much love

Whatever the thing you wish to say, there is but one word to express it, but one word to give it movement, but one adjective to qualify it; you must seek until you find this noun, this verb, this adjective

(Gustave Flaubert)

Only big words for ordinary things on account of the sound
(Leopold Bloom)

Contents

Preface

This book is about a form of the English language which is both quite distinct and very widely used: Standard Written English, the formal version of the written language, which differs from informal written English, and from the various sorts of spoken English, and which is common to the whole of the English-speaking world.

Part I, about the English language itself, concerns its elements: vocabulary, grammar, usage, and so on. Then Part II shows how these elements can be put together in the formal written language. Parts III and IV contain examples of Standard Written English in actual use, with commentaries, which illustrate and enlarge on what has been proposed in the first two Parts: Part III follows the work of four notable stylists, and Part IV is a collection of fifty case studies in the use of the language arranged by subjects.

Standard Written English: A Guide is thus both a manual for those who want to master Standard Written English, and a collection of annotated illustrations to help them on their way. The book ends with an article on the history of the English language by the lexicographer Dr R. W. Burchfield, and an annotated bibliography.

Acknowledgements

Jackie Jones, the Editorial Director of Edinburgh University Press, suggested that I should write this book, and she has been generous with advice and practical assistance while it was being written; I am most grateful to her. I would also like to thank Alison Sproston, Sub-Librarian of Trinity College, Cambridge, for answering my frequent calls for help with her usual good nature; Margaret Gaskell and Ella Westland for reading the typescript and making valuable suggestions; and Dr R. W. Burchfield for kindly allowing me to reprint his article 'The Story of the English Language' as an appendix.

COPYRIGHT ACKNOWLEDGEMENTS

Grateful acknowledgement is made to the following sources for permission to reproduce material in this book previously published elsewhere. Every effort has been made to trace copyright holders but if any have been inadvertently overlooked the publisher will be pleased to make the necessary arrangement at the first opportunity.

Bertrand Russell, from *The Problems of Philosophy*, 1980; Robert Burchfield (ed.), from *The New Fowler's Modern English Usage*, 1996; Robert Burchfield, from *The English Language*, 1985; Chris Baldick, from *The Concise Oxford Dictionary of Literary Terms*, Clarendon Press, 1990; Mary Warnock, from *Ethics Since 1900*, 2nd edition, 1966; A. J. P. Taylor, from *English History 1914–1945*, London: Pelican, 1973. Used by permission of Oxford University Press.

Virginia Woolf, from *To the Lighthouse*, London: Hogarth Press, 1927 and from *Three Guineas*, London: Hogarth Press, 1938.

Used by permission of The Society of Authors as the Literary Representative of the Estate of Virginia Woolf.

Anthony Powell, from *Hearing Secret Harmonies*, London: Heinemann, 1975. Used by permission of David Higham Associates.

Richard Pipes, from *Russia under the Bolshevik Regime*, Harvill & HarperCollins, 1994. Reproduced by permission of HarperCollins*Publishers*.

Orlando Figes, from *A People's Tragedy: the Russian Revolution 1891–1924*, London: Jonathan Cape, 1996; Aldous Huxley, from *The Perennial Philosophy*, London: Chatto and Windus, 1946. Used by permission of Random House.

Sir David Cecil, from *Early Victorian Novelists*, Penguin, 1948. Used by permission of Constable Publishers.

Peter Marsh, Elizabeth Rosser, Rom Harré, from *The Rules of Disorder*, 1987; Otto Fenichel, from *The Psychoanalytic Theory of Neurosis*, 1990. Reproduced by permission of Routledge.

Richard L. Hills, from *Power from Wind: a History of Windmill Technology*, 1994. Used by permission of Cambridge University Press.

The publishers wish to thank Oxford University Press for permission to reprint 'The Story of the English Language' by R. W. Burchfield from *Oxford English: A Guide to the Language*, compiled by I. C. B. Dear, Oxford University Press 1986.

Abbreviations

AmE	American English
BrE	British English
COD	*The Concise Oxford Dictionary of Current English*
Collins	*Collins English Dictionary*
L.	Latin
ME	Middle English
medL	medieval Latin
modE	modern English
modF	modern French
New Fowler	*The New Fowler's Modern English Usage,* 3rd edn
OE	Old English
OED	*The Oxford English Dictionary*
OF	Old French
ON	Old Norse
SWE	Standard Written English

Part I
The English Language

1 STANDARD WRITTEN ENGLISH

Language as raw material

Language is the writer's basic raw material, rather as musical notes and musical instruments are the musician's raw material, or as coloured shapes on a two-dimensional surface are the painter's raw material. And, just as the musician has to learn to read and play music, and the painter has to learn how to draw, to mix colours, and to wield a brush, so the writer has to learn how to make language say just what he or she wants it to say.

Although almost everyone can speak their own language, with more or less competence, not everyone masters the different skills of writing it effectively. Even those who can write well in a particular style – as writers of engaging personal letters, say, or of lively paragraphs in a periodical – may not be so good at writing in other styles. The analogy with music and painting can be taken further here. Considering them as craftsmen, competent composers can write music in different ways to suit different occasions and different instrumentations, producing symphonies, string quartets, songs, piano sonatas, and musical jokes in a variety of styles. Similarly, the methods of well-trained painters will vary as they produce images ranging from large canvases to small vignettes, as well as photographs, book covers, advertisements, cartoons, and stage sets. Thus good writers, as craftsmen, can use language in different ways for different applications, varying their styles to produce anything in a range from formal essays through ephemeral journalism to personal letters.

Written English

Most people are equipped by their education to write in a simple way that can be used in school compositions and personal letters; but a formal style that is appropriate for publication in books and journals, or for written work in a professional organisation – such as the office of anything from a small business to a multi-national corporation, a government department, or an educational institution – may have to be learned, or relearned. This formal style is Standard Written English (hereafter SWE). To be able to write SWE is not only an invaluable skill in itself, but it has the further advantage of being the basis for the formation of any other style that the writer wants to use; as with so many activities, you have to know the rules to be able to break them.

Standard English

English is spoken all over the world in a wide variety of dialects, and there is no one variety of spoken English that can properly be described as 'standard'. Professional linguists[1] have argued for some time that all languages, in whatever dialect, are as good and useful as each other, and that the very concept of 'standard English' is flawed. This may be true as far as the spoken language is concerned (though other linguists dispute it[2]); but there can be no doubt that *SWE, an international standard form of written English, does actually exist,* whatever the linguists say, and that it is in constant, widespread use. It is the form used by those for whom writing is a part of their professional life, whether or not they learned English as their first language; it is the form used for such things as works of scholarship and reference, encyclopedias, literary essays, textbooks, and official reports, and for the paper traffic of effective business and good government. (It is a form which is also used by creative writers, though their work commonly includes elements of the spoken language and of other forms peculiar to fiction, poetry, and drama.)

---

1. Strictly speaking they should be called 'linguisticians', but they dislike the term, and I shall call them 'linguists' here.
2. See John Honey, *Language is Power: The Story of Standard English and its Enemies*, 1997, which bravely argues against the levellers that there should be – and is – both a spoken and a written standard English.

SWE: *an international form*

While users of SWE may speak, and perhaps write informally, in ways that vary considerably from each other, the style of their formal writing is as a rule little affected by their nationality. To take the two major branches of the language, British English (BrE) and American English (AmE), we all know that there are a few differences between them of spelling (such as *colour/color*), vocabulary (*pavement/sidewalk*), idioms (*at a loose end/at loose ends*), verb formations (*got/gotten*), and grammar (*don't let's do it/let's don't do it*). In the spoken language, such differences combine with accent and usage to make two obviously distinct dialects, even when used by educated speakers; but when differences of spelling are edited out of the formal written language it can be very difficult to tell British SWE from American SWE – or, come to that, from the SWE of Canadians, South Africans, Australians, New Zealanders, or non-native speakers who write English fluently (see pp. 107–9 below).

Four propositions

This book, then, takes as its first proposition:

1. that SWE exists, and that it is worth an English-speaker's while to learn how to use it.

Three further propositions are added to this, which I will state baldly here, and explain and illustrate later, especially in Parts III and IV. These other propositions are:

2. that even the most abstruse concepts can be expounded in language so simple, clear, and free of unnecessary jargon that anyone who is capable of comprehending the subject can follow it without difficulty;
3. that the written language, just as much as the spoken language, is not static but changes and develops; and
4. that each person's prose style can be as individual and attractive – or unattractive – as any other facet of his or her personality.

Meanwhile we must consider in Part I some of the technicalities of formal English over which even a native speaker can stumble: vocabulary; grammar; basic usage; and the conventions of punctuation, spelling, and so on.

2   VOCABULARY

The vocabulary of a language is its total word-stock, and a personal vocabulary is the total of words that a person can recognise and – not quite the same thing – use effectively. Personal vocabularies are usually much larger than people think, running to several – probably many – tens of thousands of words. This depends, obviously, on how 'word' is defined: whether for instance each part of a verb (*love, loving, loves, loved*) is counted as a separate word, or how the multiple idiomatic uses of some words are counted (for instance, *turn about, turn away, turn back, turn off, turn-off, turn on, turn-on, turn out, turn-out, turn over, turnover, turn round, turn-round, turn turtle, turn up*, and many other idioms, each with a word-like meaning, based on 'turn').

Writers must master the vocabulary appropriate to what they want to write. It is difficult to define exactly what this involves in the case of SWE, but it would include (1) the 3,000 or so words taught for elementary English as a foreign language, plus a further 3,000 that a native speaker would normally use; (2) idiomatic usages, phrasal verbs, compounds, and so on, which might multiply these totals by a factor of anything from five to ten; and (3) such less common words not already counted which are used in broadsheet newspapers, news magazines, literary reviews and literary criticism, works of general history, biographies, parliamentary reports, and so on. This gives a total of at least 50,000 words and word-like items of vocabulary. (The total word-stock of the English language is calculated by some to be as many as 500,000 words and word-like formations.) In addition to this general word-stock, individual writers of SWE will also use the special vocabularies (or jargons) of their particular subjects; more will be said about this in section 4 below on usage.

If one's vocabulary is found occasionally to be inadequate for SWE, the only solution is to read widely and to use a good dictionary to look up the meaning of every word that one is not sure of; and at the same time to make lists of particularly difficult words. Here is a specimen list of ninety-five words, together with sentences to explain them, which are commonly used in SWE but which are sometimes misunderstood or confused:

abrogate/arrogate (verbs[3])

> *The old statute was abrogated and a new one substituted for it/He arrogated to himself an undeserved dignity*

abysmal/abyssal

> *The quality of his work was abysmal, and he failed his exams/The abyssal deeps of the ocean plunge down further from sea level than the greatest mountains rise above it*

access/accession (verbs)

> *The files cannot be accessed without a password/The books have to be accessioned before they can be borrowed from the library*

aggravate (verb)

> *His discomfort was aggravated by the heat/She was aggravated by her child's misbehaviour* (the second usage is now more acceptable in SWE than it used to be)

all together/altogether (adverbs)

> *We sat all together at the back of the hall/but altogether it was a disappointing lecture*

alternate/alternative (adjectives)

> *The cliff showed alternate layers of limestone and shale/The alternative proposal was the better one*

amend/emend (of documents; verbs)

> *The statute is unworkable and is to be amended/Many of the corruptions in Shakespeare's plays have been emended by textual scholars*

ante-/anti- (prefixes)

> *We entered the anteroom before reaching the mess proper/The anti-nuclear protesters blew up the power station*

appraise/apprise (verbs)

> *She appraised both his intelligence and his potential value to the company/and she then apprised her fellow-directors of his appointment*

billion/trillion (nouns and adjectives)

> AmE usage *billion = one thousand million, 10^9*, is superseding BrE *one million million, 10^{12}*; and AmE *trillion =*

---

3. For the meaning of 'verb', 'noun', 'adjective', and so on, see p. 12 below.

one million million, 10^{12}, is superseding BrE *one million million million,* 10^{18}

celibate/chaste (adjectives)

Although they had sex together, they remained celibate (= unmarried)/*Although they were married, they remained chaste* (= did not have sex together; but 'celibate' is also used loosely to mean 'chaste')

centenary/centennial (nouns)

both words are now used for *hundredth anniversary*; but 'centennial' can still have its original adjectival meaning of *every hundred years*

complacent/complaisant (adjectives)

His smile was smugly complacent as he accepted the prize/*She asked for help and, complaisant, he was glad to give it*

consist in/consist of (verbs)

My happiness consists in the existence of my family/*My family consists of my wife and two children*

convince (verb)

BrE and AmE *I am convinced* (= persuaded) *that he will come*/AmE *I will convince* (= persuade) *him to come*

decimate (verb; the imprecise meaning is now common)

(precise) *The hundred soldiers were decimated, ninety of them being left alive*/(imprecise) *The hundred soldiers were decimated, scarcely a dozen of them being left alive*

deduce, deduction/induce, induction (verbs and nouns)

All railway-engine drivers are men, so I deduce that the driver of that particular railway engine is a man, not a woman/*I have seen only male railway-engine drivers, and none that was female, therefore my induction is that all railway-engine drivers are men* ('induce' also = *prevail on, persuade*)

definite/definitive (adjectives)

His partner has definite news that he is dead/*The definitive obituary will be written by his partner*

deprecate/depreciate (verbs)

She deprecated the incompetent way in which the furniture was repaired/*The value of the furniture depreciated as a result of the incompetent way in which it was repaired* ('depreciate' also = *undervalue, disparage*) discomfit/discomfort (verbs)

I was discomfited to discover that I had foolishly let the fire go out/I was discomforted by the lack of warmth from the fire

disinterested/uninterested (adjectives)

The judge was disinterested in the case that she was trying/but she was not uninterested in its progress

eclectic (adjective)

His religious practices were eclectic, deriving from Buddhist, Hindu, and Islamic traditions as well as from Christianity

egregious (adjective)

The bank manager's egregious and unforgivable dishonesty led to the collapse of many small businesses

epicene (adjective)

Short hair, imperceptible breasts, and broad hips gave the women athletes an epicene appearance

esoteric/exoteric (adjectives)

The esoteric part of the teaching was understood only by the inner circle of disciples/while the exoteric part was available to everyone

exceptionable, unexceptionable/exceptional, unexceptional (adjectives)

His drunken antics were exceptionable/but, sober, he was seen to be an exceptional man/Her clothes were unexceptionable, and indeed quite smart/but nothing else distinguished this unexceptional woman

exegesis (noun)

The text was obscure to us at first, but the professor's brilliant exegesis made everything plain

exigent (adjective)

The teacher was exigent in her requirement that all essays be handed in on time

exiguous (adjective)

They invited me to dine, but the portions were exiguous and I was as hungry after the meal as I had been before

explanation/explication (nouns)

He gave a satisfactory explanation of why he had missed the meeting/Her clear explication of the document was a great help to them all fictitious/factitious/factious (adjectives)

Mr Bunbury, a useful but fictitious character, could never appear on the stage/His anger was factitious and put on for the occasion, while he concealed his real feelings/The barracking from the Opposition benches was merely factious and expressed no disagreement of principle

fulsome (adjective)

The praise was so fulsome as to offend him with its cloying excess (but 'fulsome' is also used loosely in a favourable sense, especially in AmE, so that 'fulsome praise' = 'high praise' or 'copious praise')

hopefully (adverb)

see below

human (noun)

see below

hyper-/hypo- (prefixes)

The hypertensive patient, who was about to burst a blood vessel,/was given drugs to produce a condition of hypotension, thus avoiding the threatened stroke

immanent/imminent (adjectives)

We believe that the love of God is immanent, within us and without,/but we cannot hope, with the millenarians, that His reincarnation is imminent

inchoate (adjective)

Her last book was found to be inchoate at the time of her death, and it was completed for publication by her colleagues

infer/imply (verbs)

I inferred from the slurring of his speech that he was drunk/even though he implied, without actually saying so, that he had taken nothing stronger than tea

inter-/intra- (prefixes)

The UN is an international organisation which promotes harmony between nations/This is the syringe which the intravenous drug-user stuck into his vein

jejune (adjective)

His jejune remarks showed him to be a naive intellectual lightweight

leading question (noun)

You shot your wife, didn't you? is a leading question because it leads the witness to answer 'yes'/but *Did you*

shoot your wife? is not leading
livid (adjective)
> *His face was quite red with anger, but hers was livid, a
> leaden, deathly hue* (also used loosely to mean 'angry')

misanthropist/misogynist (nouns)
> *That wretched misanthropist hates everyone/but at least
> his brother, who is only a misogynist, likes men*

mutual (adjective)
> see pp. 85–7 below

paradigm/parameter (nouns)
> *The federal government and the individual states serve
> as a paradigm of the relationship between university and
> colleges at Oxbridge/The debate took place within the
> parameters that had been accepted by both sides*

periphrasis (noun)
> *In elegant periphrasis she conveyed her meaning without
> actually saying the uncomfortable words*

picaresque (adjective)
> *This novel is indeed episodic, but – lacking rogues and
> scoundrels – it cannot be described as picaresque*

prevaricate/procrastinate (verbs)
> *Unable to make up his mind, he prevaricated, favouring
> first one solution, then another/Unable to make up his
> mind, he procrastinated until there was no more time for
> discussion*

regretfully/regrettably (adverbs)
> *The invitation was declined – regretfully, for she had
> wanted to come/The invitation was accepted but, regret-
> tably, she failed to appear*

satire/satyr (nouns)
> *It is a satire ridiculing the life and loves of Frank
> Harris/the would-be satyr who hoped that no innocent
> was safe from his sensuality*

semantic (adjective)
> *A large part of the appeal of Eliot's poetry is semantic,
> deriving from its meaning as much as from its sound*

sinecure/cynosure (nouns)
> *I took the job, believing that it was a sinecure and that I
> should not be required to do anything/The fact that he
> took the money and did nothing for it did not distress his
> mother, for he was the cynosure of her eyes*

supercargo (noun)
> *He was appointed supercargo for the return voyage, but there was in fact no cargo to look after as the ship was in ballast*

super-/supra- (prefixes)
> *The appeal of Superman transcends all boundaries, and is indeed supranational*

temporal/temporary (adjectives)
> *The vicar's fund-raising became so important to him that he cared more for temporal than for spiritual affairs/but when he reached his financial target this proved to have been a temporary aberration*

venal/venial (adjectives)
> *A venal policeman was paid to destroy the evidence/but taking a bribe is not considered to be a venial offence in the police force*

Here it is well to remember proposition 3: that the written language, just as much as the spoken language, is not static but changes and develops. It accepts change, moreover, at different speeds, as can be seen with the words 'human', 'privatisation', and 'hopefully'. 'Human', used as a noun as a short form of 'human being', has a history going back to the sixteenth century, but it is only now that it is making its way into SWE (*it was obviously a human habitation, but there were no humans in sight*). On the other hand 'privatisation', meaning the opposite of 'nationalisation',[4] first appeared as recently as 1969, but was accepted for use in SWE within a decade (*New Labour does not oppose the privatisation of several of the remaining nationalised industries*). As for 'hopefully', before the 1930s in America, and before the 1970s in Britain, the word meant only *doing something with hope* (*to travel hopefully is better than to arrive*); but now it is most frequently used in spoken English to mean *it is to be hoped that* (*hopefully I shall arrive tomorrow*). The second meaning, which tends to be disliked by older speakers, has not yet penetrated far into SWE; but the two meanings are usually distinguishable in context, and we can be fairly sure that 'hopefully' as a concise way of saying *it is to be hoped that* will quite

---

4. 'Privatisation' has another, different, meaning in the jargon of the social sciences.

soon be part of SWE (where it will join the similar use of 'happily': *the children played happily together/happily the children did not hit each other*).[5]

A few other points.

1. *a* or *an* before initials or acronyms: follow the pronunciation; for instance write *an RAF man*, even though the expanded form is *a Royal Air Force man*.
2. Although *alright* is normally an impermissible (demotic) spelling of *all right*, it could conceivably be used in dialogue to distinguish *his answers were all right* from *his answers were good ones alright*.
3. *it's* and *its* are not interchangeable (*it's a good thing that the lorry didn't shed its load*).
4. *Elision* (the colloquial contraction of *I will* to *I'll*, *did not* to *didn't*, *do not* to *don't*, and so on) is rare in SWE, though there is no reason why it should not be used occasionally if it fits the tone of what is being written.[6]

It is also important in practice – because SWE is likely to be submitted for duplication or publication – to know how to spell correctly, and for those whose spelling is shaky it is best to get help, either from a friend or from the spellcheck program of a word-processor.

Note that there are spelling variations in BrE, such as:

> *connection/connexion* (a matter of printer's or publisher's 'house style', but the former spelling is now generally preferred)
> *disc/disk* ('disk' was until recently an AmE spelling, but it is now commonly used in BrE in connection with computers; similarly *programme* [BrE] and *program* [AmE, and in BrE in connection with computers])
> *gaol/jail* ('gaol' has been the normal spelling in BrE, but is now giving way to 'jail' which is used in AmE, Australian English, and so on)
> *judgement/judgment* ('judgement' is normally preferred, but 'judgment' is used in legal contexts)
> *theorise/theorize* (there are words which must end in *-ise*;

5. See also the changing meanings of 'mutual', pp. 85–7 below.
6. See also p. 24 below, 'apostrophe'.

others which must end in *-ize*; and others again which may end in either [when *-ize* is preferred in AmE]. See the lists in Burchfield's *New Fowler* s.v. -ise, -ize)

There are also of course many well-known differences of spelling between BrE and AmE, such as: *centre/center*; *favour/favor*; *tyre/tire*, and so on. See also section 5 below, on the conventions of punctuation and layout.

3   GRAMMAR

Grammar is a way of analysing and describing how the words of a language are used in relation to each other to convey meaning. We understand the common terms that refer to parts of speech – nouns, verbs, adjectives, and so on – in a sentence such as:

The	*handsome*	*boy*	*quickly*	*gives*	*a*	*flower*
article	adjective	noun	adverb	verb	article	noun

to	*her,*	*and*	*Fido*	*barks.*
preposition	pronoun	conjunction	proper noun	verb

We are also aware of some simple rules for their relationship, such as that a singular subject is followed by a singular, not a plural, verb, so that we could not say *The handsome boy quickly give a flower to her*; and that when a pronoun is the subject of a sentence it takes the subject case (*I, he, she, we, they*), but when it is the object of a preposition, it takes the object case (*me, him, her, us, them*), so that *The handsome boy quickly gives a flower to she* would also be wrong.

Of course English grammar has many more rules and conventions than this, and it is hard for non-native speakers to master its finer points. Some grammatical rules, and the jargon in which they are expressed, can seem difficult even for native speakers, but there is no need to be alarmed because we learned as small children how the grammar of our native language works in practice, and we do not need to know how to describe it technically. In nearly every case a grammatical puzzle can be solved by letting our feeling for the language take charge; the rule is simply: *Go for what sounds right.*

What we mean when we speak of our own or someone else's 'bad grammar' is usually no more than a small number of common mistakes of form and usage, which occur more often in speech than in writing, and which are relatively easy to put right; things such as case and number confusions, double possessives, false subjunctives, misplaced apostrophes, and so on. Here are some examples, with the right form immediately following the wrong one:

> number (changing number during a sentence)
>> *There is likely to be differences between us/There are likely ...*
>> *The last crop to be harvested were potatoes/ ... was potatoes*
>> *The BBC does their classic drama very well/... does its ...* (or ... *do their* ... if the BBC is taken to be a plural noun)

> case (especially with pronouns)
>> *They kindly invited my husband and I to dinner/my husband and me ...* (the way to test this one is to leave out 'my husband and', whereupon it is obvious that *They kindly invited I to dinner* is wrong)
>> *Between you and I/Between you and me*
>> *It might have been him and not the Prime Minister who made the speech / ... been he and ...*
>> *I am afraid that the culprit is me/ ... is I*; or better still rearranged as *I am afraid that I am the culprit* (though *It's me, That's him,* and so on, are good colloquial English)
>> *Who shall he give it to?/Whom shall he give it to?*
>> *Yet the final arbiter be whom he may/ ... be who he may*

> possessives (double possessives; apostrophes)
>> *He praised the eccentric novel of Sterne's/*(this has to be recast as) *He praised Sterne's eccentric novel* (but *He praised an* [or *this*] *eccentric novel of Sterne's* is right)
>> The following forms are all correct: *The Jones family/ Keeping up with the Joneses/The Joneses' house/Mrs Jones's dress*

> subjunctives (false subjunctives with *if*)
>> *If he were there, he was in the wrong place/If he was there ...*
>> *If the vote is close, and if a recount be demanded, he will retire/ ... if a recount is demanded, ...*

obsolete conjugations (dost, doth, and so on)
> *Dost he attend the court?/Doth he attend the court?*
> *Thou understandeth not/Thou understandest not*
> *She givest of her best/She giveth of her best*

Seven other grammatical points that can cause trouble may be mentioned here. They are:

(1) *The 'shall' and 'will' rule*

In the first person the auxiliary verb *shall (do something)* expresses the simple future: *I shall/we shall (do something).* In the second and third persons, however, the simple future is expressed by *will: you will/he will/she will/it will/they will (do something).* When these persons and auxiliaries are exchanged, however, an intention or determination is expressed. *I will do it* means that I am determined to do it; *she shall be paid* means, not just that payment is going to be made, but that there is a definite intention to pay her.

A native speaker from England will probably follow this rule correctly – at least in writing – without thinking about it; but he or she may run into trouble in, say, Scotland or America, where the rule is commonly reversed. Thus the simple future of *This too will pass* (BrE) becomes *This too shall pass* (AmE); while the Englishman drowning in Scottish waters who shouts in panic 'No-one will save me, I shall drown!' may seem to the locals to be saying that no-one wants to save him and that he is determined to drown. In ordinary speech, however, intention is more often expressed by stressing the auxiliary, when either *will* or *shall* can be used, and the simple future by elision (*I'll do it*).

(2) *Unattached (or misrelated or hanging) participles*

A participle, with a verb ending in *-ed, -ing*, and so on, may be used as an adjectival or descriptive phrase preceding the main subject of a sentence, as in *Pleased with the new chapter, I stopped work and had a cup of tea*; here it is clearly 'I' who is pleased. But if the participle refers to something other than the main subject, it is unattached and can mislead: *Covered with the copy-editor's annotations, I thought it best to rewrite the new chapter* – where it is not 'I' but 'the new chapter' that is covered with the copy-editor's annotations.

(3) *Managing without a gender-free personal pronoun*

In the past, 'he' (like 'man' or 'mankind') could be used in general contexts to refer to men and women taken together (*When a passenger is asked for a ticket he must produce one*); but this is no longer as acceptable as it was. Unfortunately English has no singular personal pronoun that refers jointly to male and female, so that we must either say *When a passenger is asked for a ticket he or she must produce one*; or put the whole thing in the plural and say *When passengers are asked for tickets, they must produce them*; or use an ugly and unpronounceable neologism such as *s/he*. 'He or she' and 'his or hers' can sound fussy if they are used too often; while to substitute 'they' for 'he or she' (or 'their' for 'his or hers'), when the subject is unambiguously in the singular, requires an awkward change of number; and there is in fact no solution to the problem that is as neat as the old one of using 'he' to stand for 'he or she'.

(4) *'Whose' with a non-personal antecedent*

Items (4) to (7) in this group are grammarian's rules which have little point to them in the real world of SWE; there is no good reason why they should not be broken occasionally, though it is often difficult for older people to break them without a sense of guilt. In this case, I was taught at school that 'whose' could only be used to refer to persons (or, at a pinch, animals); so that you could write *The girls, whose summer dresses brightened the morning*, but not *The streets, whose decorations brightened the morning*. 'Whose' has been used with non-personal antecedents for centuries (*Of man's first disobedience, and the fruit / Of that forbidden tree, whose taste / Brought death into the world ...*[7]), and there can be no real objection to it.

(5) *Beginning sentences with 'And' or 'But'*

The reason for objecting to this practice was presumably that a sentence was considered to be a closed unit of meaning, whereas 'and' and 'but' were conjunctions which necessarily joined one

---

7. Note also, in connection with gender-free language, that Milton writes of 'man's' disobedience even though it was Eve who actually tasted the fruit.

part of an incomplete sentence to another. The prohibition has been ignored by good writers throughout the history of the language from Anglo-Saxon times, and there is no need to observe it today.

(6) *Ending sentences with prepositions*

The 'rule' that sentences should not be ended with prepositions was first suggested by Dryden in 1672, but it has never been consistently obeyed; indeed ending a sentence with a preposition is often unavoidable, as in *What did they talk about?* (it would be absurd to write *About what did they talk?*); or at least desirable, as in *There was a man she was attracted by* (where *There was a man by whom she was attracted* might seem too formal). Again, do it if it sounds right.

(7) *Splitting infinitives*

We come, finally, to this oldest of grammatical disputes – for infinitives have been regularly split, and regularly objected to, for centuries. I have to admit that I have been so conditioned that I still cannot comfortably write *To clearly understand* ..., and that I am disturbed to see that it is the task of the Starship 'Enterprise' *to boldly go* ...; but I also know that there is no respectable authority for my discomfort. If splitting an infinitive can enhance meaning without awkwardness, then let it be split.

To sum up, practitioners of SWE who are educated native speakers should have no real difficulty with grammar, and their copy-editors will certainly correct them if they make a grammatical mistake.[8]

4   USAGE

Sentences made from a large stock of words arranged in the proper grammatical relationships will not necessarily result in the form of SWE that the writer wants to achieve; there are also the questions of choosing the right words for the job, and of arranging them in ways that are easy and pleasant to read. Questions of English usage in its broader sense will be addressed

8. On copy-editing, see pp. 39–40 below.

in Part II. This section is concerned with a number of relatively minor but often awkward points of usage which had better be dealt with first.

Special vocabularies, slang, and jargons

Groups of people which have separate identities, of age or calling or way of life, communicate within the group, both in speech and in writing, by using language with a special vocabulary that is appropriate to each one. Thus schoolchildren at play have a special vocabulary; so do literary critics, theatre people, stockbrokers, football fans, scientists, politicians, jazz musicians, policemen, gays, teenagers, poets, and any number of others. Not only do members of particular groups use their special vocabularies in talking to each other, but writings addressed to them, such as specialist books, journals, and magazines, also use these vocabularies to a greater or lesser extent.

When a special vocabulary becomes markedly informal it can slip into colloquial slang, when it may be almost incomprehensible to outsiders. Slang is unlikely to be used in SWE except to make a relevant point, though some special subjects – genetics, say, or musical composition – cannot be discussed in SWE without the use of a number of specialist terms. As far as possible such specialist terms should be familiar to educated readers; otherwise they can be defined as they occur.

Besides slipping into informality and slang, specialist writing can also cloak itself in the obscurity of unrelieved jargon, a formal but extreme special vocabulary comprehensible only to initiates, so dense that it can even trap its practitioners into writing nonsense. Among subjects which are particularly beset by jargon of this sort are the social sciences, linguistics, criticism, some natural sciences, and some branches of philosophy. Here is a paragraph that explains certain developments in post-structuralist linguistics, using the jargon of the subject; it is obviously not nonsense, but parts of it are nevertheless almost incomprehensible to anyone not acquainted with its specialist vocabulary:

> Julia Kristeva, though associated with structuralism, like Barthes eventually moved beyond it. For her, like Derrida, the emphasis is on the signifier rather than the signified in

> language, as the signifying process undermines all stability
> of meaning. The signifying process both creates and under-
> mines systems of signs. Influenced by both psychoanalysis
> and Bakhtin, she stresses the role of the 'speaking subject'
> in language with the subject being always divided because
> the 'other' cannot be eliminated from the discourse. She
> suggests that in modernist literary writing language can
> be a force for renewal since modernist literary language
> both creates and calls into question systematisation. (K. M.
> Newton, *Twentieth Century Literary Theory: A Reader*,
> 2nd edn, Macmillan, London 1997, p. 113)

As my second proposition suggested, and as will be demonstrated in Parts III and IV, even the most abstruse concepts can
be expounded in language so simple, clear, and free of unnecessary jargon that anyone who is capable of comprehending the
subject can follow it without difficulty. Note the word 'unnecessary' here: abstruse concepts are usually going to need some
specialist jargon for their explication; but the jargon must be
explained, kept under strict control, and used in a framework of
simple language.

Idioms

Idioms are groups of words which, in association with each other,
have meanings not deducible from the individual words. Thus
carry the can, *get the sack*, *kick the bucket* are widely understood
idioms in BrE which no longer have anything to do with carrying
literal cans, receiving literal sacks, or kicking literal buckets.
English is indeed extremely rich in idioms which make up much
of its astonishing diversity. A majority of them, perhaps, are more
colloquial than formal, like these three dead metaphors; but there
are still many that are an essential part of SWE.

Some are relatively simple but required uses of prepositions
(we have to say *insensible to* but *unconscious of*, and *for long* but
at length); others are set phrases (*odds and ends*, *ups and downs*,
ins and outs are examples that could be used in SWE); others
again are the numerous and varied meanings that can be derived
from a single word, and which are an integral part of the
language. Some of the idiomatic uses of the word 'turn' have been
mentioned already (p. 4 above); here is another group of idioms

that uses the word 'hand': *all hands, at first hand, by hand, change hands, a dab hand, a free hand, in hand, off hand, hands off, hands up, high hand, take in hand, to hand, under hand, the upper hand*, and dozens of others based on 'hand'.[9]

Rhetorical stress, where we stress a particular word (of one or more syllables) to indicate our meaning, also has an idiomatic dimension. In speaking, if the phrase 'scalding pan' is stressed on the first word it means a special sort of pan used for scalding milk in a dairy; but if is stressed on the second word it means a pan – any sort of pan – that is scalding hot. Again, a simple sentence can have as many different meanings as there are words in it; for instance, the six-word sentence 'Where can I sleep well tonight?' can be spoken without extra stress on any particular word as a plain, unweighted question about where I am going to sleep well; or it can be given any of six additional, special meanings by putting extra stress onto each of its six words in turn: 'Whére can I sleep well tonight?', 'Where cán I sleep well tonight?', 'Where can Í sleep well tonight?', and so on.

Native speakers of English are fortunate that its idioms are learned without effort when they are young, for they are central to the understanding and use of the language, yet are not easy for non-native speakers to master. Idioms will be in constant play by writers of SWE, who should not be shy of using even colloquial ones in the right places.

Figures of speech

In general, rhetorical figures of speech should never be obtrusive in SWE; they are seldom really necessary, and if they are obvious they are more likely to put readers off than to help them on. Nevertheless some of the less noticeable figures are worth mentioning.

(1) *Similes and metaphors*: Similes, introduced by 'like' or 'as', suggest that one thing is like something else (*The Duchess, like a great ship, sailed into the room*); metaphors make an imaginative substitution of one thing by another (*An iron curtain has descended across the Continent*). There are traps to be avoided –

9. David Crystal's *Cambridge Encyclopedia of the English Language*, 1995, p. 163, gives a list, 'which makes no claim to completeness', of over *eighty* different idioms deriving from *hand* and *hands*.

similes that are ridiculous, similes and metaphors that are self-conscious or go on too long, metaphors that are mixed or otherwise spoiled – and the best rule here is to *keep it simple*.[10]

It is worth remembering that many ordinary words that have a metaphorical content – words with an underlying, often older, meaning that denotes, or once denoted, something else – are a part of our everyday language; and we use them without noticing that we are doing so. Consider the following extract from an article about the Conservative Party Conference of 1997, in which those words having some metaphorical content are italicised:

> Labour was *saddled* with opposing privatisation on principle, opposing *cut*-price council house sales on principle, and repeating and *entrenching* an outdated *position* on disarmament *inherited* from another *age*. They were even *stuck with* recommending *withdrawal* from the European Community. Quotes from that time are still *hurled* at them to this day, and still *sting*. (*The Times*)

Or this from a popular handbook on philosophy: 'Rights cannot be arbitrarily *overridden*, or *weighed* against the *profit* of ignoring them. Duties cannot be arbitrarily *set aside* or *cancelled* by the bad *results* of due obedience' (Roger Scruton). Or this from the dust-jacket of Burchfield's *New Fowler*: 'Let me *beg* readers as well as writers to *keep* the revised Fowler *at their elbows*. It *brims* with useful information.'

(2) *Antithesis*, placing opposites beside each other, can be used to point a contrast, both in idioms (*the long and the short of it*), and in developing an idea (*Marriage has many pains, but celibacy has no pleasures*). The engaging double antithesis of this last example is by Samuel Johnson, who also specialised in a form of extended antithesis by balancing long clauses against each other, a dignified and often pleasing eighteenth-century style that would seem contrived nowadays.

(3) *Irony*, in the form in which what is said is different from – or even the opposite of – what is meant, can be as effective a device in SWE as it is in conversation. People say *Wonderful!*

10. The best description of metaphors and their dangers is still that of H. W. Fowler in the first edition of *Modern English Usage*, 1926, s.v. metaphor.

when something disastrous happens, and analogous but subtler uses of irony are available to the writer. An essay on an episode in Joyce's *Ulysses* begins: *A crucial event takes place at this point in the narrative: Bloom does some work*, which delicately calls attention to the fact that hardly any of the characters in the book actually do anything that could be called work.[11] Mishandled, irony may tend towards *hyperbole*, which is the technical term for exaggeration; it is chiefly encountered in colloquial English (*a thousand pardons*; *I'm infinitely sorry*), and should normally be avoided in SWE.

Clichés and proverbial sayings

Unless they are used to make a point, clichés – mostly tired metaphors and similes – should not be used in SWE. Particularly exhausted examples are: *a bolt from the blue, as old as the hills, at the end of the day, avoid like the plague, dead as a doornail, explore every avenue, food for thought, grow like Topsy, keep a low profile, leave no stone unturned, put a good face on it, quick as a flash, stick out like a sore thumb, the calm before the storm, trouble is brewing.* There are tired non-metaphorical clichés to avoid, too, such as: *at this moment in time, far be it from me to, for love or money, from time immemorial, in this day and age, last but not least.* However, there are a few clichés, mostly of a proverbial character, that are unobjectionable because they express concisely what it would take too many words to say otherwise: *a miss is as good as a mile, better safe than sorry, better late than never, caveat emptor, easier said than done.* Useful proverbial clichés can also be referred to in abbreviated form: *a bird in the hand, a stitch in time, spilt milk, swan song, the last straw.*

Affectations

'Elegant variation' is the title of a classic article in the first edition of *Modern English Usage* on the avoidance of repetition, describing the contortions that writers can get into in order to avoid using the same word twice in the same sentence; as where Thackeray writes *careering during the season from one great*

11. See more of this essay on p. 108 below.

dinner of twenty <u>*covers*</u> *to another of eighteen* <u>*guests*</u> (Thackeray could have avoided the problem simply by omitting the word 'guests'). While repetition can be inelegant, it is so only when the word repeated is a noun, adjective, or verb that is important to the sense of the sentence, and not always then; many words such as articles, prepositions, auxiliary verbs, the verb *to be*, and so on, are neutral in this sense, and can – indeed often must – be repeated twice or more in the same sentence.

'Modish and inflated diction' (a useful phrase from *The Oxford Guide to English Usage*) involves the use of words and phrases that have been given fashionable currency by popular writers, tabloid journalists, and broadcasters in both radio and television. These include not only many clichés, but also catch phrases, vogue words, and pompous ways of saying ordinary things. Here is a selection of words and phrases to be avoided: *another ball game, bitter* (= pained or regretful), *bottom line, dichotomy, disgusting* (= outrageous), *escalate, eventuate, framework, gobsmacked* (= shocked), *interface, in the order/neighbourhood/region of, is all about, loved ones* (= relatives), *low profile, maximise, meaningful, name of the game, no way, obscene* (= objectionable), *on the back burner, ongoing, overly, pass on* (= die), *quantum jump/leap, scenario, simplistic (*= oversimplified), *syndrome, terminate, utilise, you name it.*

5   PUNCTUATION

Punctuation can affect the meaning and nuance of what is written. Obviously *the two-year-old babies* are not the same as *the two year-old babies*; and the omission of the commas drastically alters the sense of *I shot, myself, on 12 August.*

Though it is usually something of a compromise, punctuation can tend either towards a *grammatical* form, marking the construction of the sentences by clauses (suitable for explication), or towards a *rhetorical* form (suitable for dialogue), indicating how the sentences are spoken.

> *Greatly daring, he took the key from his pocket, where it had lain since the evening before, and gingerly put it into the old, unoiled lock.* (grammatical punctuation)
> *'Well – I had to do something so I ... yes I took the key out of my pocket – it had been weighing my jacket down*

since last night, and –' He paused. *'Then ... I can hardly believe I dared but I put the key, yes, actually into that old squeaky lock.'* (rhetorical punctuation)

This book tends towards grammatical punctuation.

Comma: commas are chiefly used to mark pauses, clauses, minor parentheses, and items enumerated within a sentence. It is easy to use too many or too few commas; if in doubt, the sentence should be read aloud to see where a definite pause is required to make the sense clear. (See the grammatically punctuated sentence above.) In enumerations, it is best not to omit the comma before the final *and*, which avoids confusion in lists such as *Harrods, Debenham and Freebody, Selfridges, and Marks and Spencer.*

Semicolon: best used to link two balanced sentences, or blocks of words, that are too closely related to be divided by full stops. *I hardly expected the clock to work; but, after winding it, I was rewarded by a healthy tick.*

Colon: Fowler (1926) remarks briskly that the colon has acquired the special function of delivering the goods that have been invoiced in the preceding words. *She brought her usual paraphernalia: purse, parasol, gloves, and galoshes.* Hart's *Rules* (1983) adds that it generally marks a step forward, from introduction to main theme, from cause to effect, from premiss to conclusion; though in some of these cases a semicolon, or even a comma, would do just as well. *The waiting room was for ladies only: so he supposed that he could not go in and look for her.*

Full stop: full stops, which bring sentences to an end, can be tiresome if they are used to break prose up into ridiculously short sentences, or verbless blocks of words (unless the punctuation is intended to be rhetorical). Abbreviations should be terminated with a full stop only where the abbreviated form does not end with the last letter of the full form of the word (thus *Dr, Mr, Mrs, Bart* do not have full stops; but *e.g., etc., fig., i.e., N.B.* do have them); note however that there is a modern tendency to omit full stops from all abbreviations.

Exclamation mark: used for exclamations (*oh!, damnation!*), and exclamatory sentences (*What an extraordinary thing!*), but to be avoided for marking the merely odd or funny.

Question mark: sometimes wrongly omitted because the writer has forgotten that the sentence is a question. To put either an exclamation mark or a question mark in round brackets, to indicate an authorial comment on what is said, can seem painfully arch.

Inverted commas: British editors and printers prefer single inverted commas to mark direct speech, while American ones prefer double. It does not matter which sort is used (unless work is submitted as a computer disk for making camera-ready copy), provided that the other sort is used for interior quotations.[12] A full stop (or exclamation mark or question mark) ending a sentence is sometimes placed inside closing inverted commas; otherwise punctuation marks are placed outside closing inverted commas.

Apostrophe: apostrophes should not be used to form plurals, as in the following wrong forms: *banana's 49p, the 1990's, PC's for MP's*. In direct speech, *do not*, and so on, indicates a different pronunciation, and probably a different emphasis, from *don't*, and so on. See also the notes on elisions and on possessives in section 2, pp. 11 and 13 above.

Hyphens: used in compound nouns and adjectives: *twentieth-century writers/in the twentieth century*. Note the different meanings of *a little used car* and *a little-used car*.

Italics (shown by underlining): used to mark emphasis on a particular (usually unexpected) word, or foreign words and phrases, or examples in a book such as this; but italicising whole sentences can be a mistake. Italics, not inverted commas, are used for the titles of books, inverted commas for the titles of articles.

Brackets: round brackets ( ), called parentheses, are used for parenthetical clauses that need something stronger than paired commas: *The dog was barking all night (it was of course the dog from next door) and she didn't sleep a wink*. Square brackets [] are used for parentheses inside round brackets, and also to mark material supplied editorially.

Dashes: may be used in pairs instead of round brackets for parenthetical clauses (the sentence above about the barking dog could be written with dashes in place of the round brackets). Single dashes may sometimes be used to indicate a pause in direct speech, and occasionally as a substitute for some other punctuation mark (see the next sentence).

---

12. In the book I wrote before this one, I thought I would try double quotes (as they are sometimes called); in this one I have gone back to single ones. It seems to make no difference.

Ellipses ... (three dots – not four or five): used to mark words omitted; and occasionally to indicate a pause, usually in dialogue.

Part II
Writing English

1 THE MECHANICS OF WRITING

Every writer has his or her own way of writing. Some have to write with pencil or pen (either because it is the only way that works for them, or because they cannot type), others can write straight onto a typewriter or word-processor; others again can dictate to a stenographer or tape recorder, though few can do it well.

Although secretaries[1] are trained to transcribe from manuscripts onto a keyboard, no one else will be eager nowadays to read anything written by hand; and manuscripts of works intended for publication are definitely not acceptable to publishers or their professional readers. To be able to type, whether on a typewriter or a personal computer, is as useful as being able to drive a car, and everyone should be able to type at least competently. Besides, the process of typing out a manuscript, whether of a letter or a report or an article, gives an excellent opportunity for revising it. Better still is to use a word-processor, on which the process of revision can be virtually continuous from first draft to last, and which, if the author is up to it, can produce a disk or disks to accompany the author's printout, little $3\frac{1}{2}$-inch disks which can contain as much as a whole book ready to be coded as 'camera-ready copy' without having to be transcribed again.

Organising materials, reference books, sources, and time

Obvious as it seems, the first thing to do is to see that writing

---

1. A 'secretary' used to be what is now usually called a personal assistant, and sometimes still is; but now the word is also used to mean a stenographer or copy-typist.

materials are to hand – lined paper, pencils, and eraser; or typewriter, ribbons, paper, carbons, correction fluid, and scissors and paste; or word-processor, printer ribbons, paper, and disks – in sufficient quantities. It is tiresome and ridiculous if they run out.

Then there are the three essential reference books to be kept where the writing is done: first, a really good, comprehensive dictionary, such as the latest edition of *The Concise Oxford Dictionary of Current English* (COD) or of *Collins English Dictionary* (*Collins*), not an older, shorter, or less authoritative dictionary; next R. W. Burchfield's third edition of *Fowler's Modern English Usage*, Oxford 1996 (*New Fowler*); and last, a thesaurus, or word-finder, such as the latest edition of the Penguin *Roget's Thesaurus of English Words and Phrases*, ed. Susan M. Lloyd. These three books alone will meet virtually all a writer's needs for reference as far as language is concerned.

Other books and sources will also be required, depending on what is to be written. A good biographical dictionary such as the splendid *Chambers Biographical Dictionary*, 5th edn 1990, may have to be referred to, or perhaps the *Dictionary of National Biography*, or the annual *Who's Who*. But, for the most part, different sources and reference books will be used for each particular piece of work. Ideally they should be readily available to the writer; if they are not, they must be found. Most public libraries stock encyclopedias; dictionaries and lexicons for a range of languages; dictionaries of biography by countries and professions; dictionaries of proverbs, quotations, personal names, and place names; atlases, gazetteers, local directories; and many other specialist reference books.

And finally, there is time. Different writers write at different speeds, and the result is unlikely to be good if there is not all the uninterrupted time needed to write and to revise. Professional writers often – perhaps usually – write to fixed hours every day, sometimes requiring themselves to produce a quota of words at each session. This may not be possible or even desirable when the writer is composing memoranda or reports in an office, but for articles and books written at home there is everything to be said for regular hours of writing – everything, that is, except for the sacrifice demanded of the writer's spouse and family, who usually find out that successful writing requires ruthless detachment and concentration.

Planning

A certain amount of planning in advance is essential if the writer is to avoid wasting time and effort on false starts and rewriting. There are various ways of planning a piece of written work, but the traditional, and probably most effective, method is to write a synopsis. This may be no more than a list of headings jotted on a piece of paper, or it may be something more detailed – an abstract of the argument, perhaps, with notes on the contents of each chapter or section. There is no need to regard such a plan as immutable – writing has a way of developing as it goes on, sometimes in unexpected directions – but it will still be necessary for the author to have a good idea before starting of what the report, article, or book is going to be about, and how the argument or information is to be presented and resolved; it will not matter if a few things have to be changed later. If research has to be done, scrupulous notes, with references, should be kept; there is nothing more maddening, when the writing is going well, than half-remembering some vital piece of information but not remembering where to find it. One point here, small but important: quotations and references should always be verified, preferably at source, never taken from memory alone.

Provided that the plan of the projected work is clearly worked out, there is no absolute need to write it in order from beginning to end. This is usually the most convenient thing to do; but there may be reasons – such as the temporary unavailability of information – that make it more sensible to write chapters or sections out of order.[2]

2 WORDS

In Part I we saw how large is the word-stock available to the writer, and considered a number of words, idioms, locutions, and usages that are better avoided. But knowing what not to say is the easy part; what is difficult is choosing the right words for the job from the huge number of words that are the synonyms or near-synonyms of other words, or which have extremely subtle shades of meaning. Words, moreover, may be emotive or neutral;

2. It happened with this book that I started with Part I, then compiled two-thirds of the examples and commentaries in Part IV, then went on to Part II, then wrote Part III, and finally finished off Part IV.

they may contain class-indicators; they may be politically correct or incorrect; they may mean different things in different contexts.

One way of looking at the problem is to suppose that for every important word – usually a main noun, a main verb, an adjective, or an adverb, but not a subsidiary noun or adjective, a pronoun, an auxiliary verb, a preposition, or a conjunction – there is one, and only one, perfect choice. This may or not be true in particular circumstances, but if we accept that it is at least possibly true, we shall be wary of making the thoughtless, easy choice; and we shall pause (if only for a moment) at every word we write to ask ourselves, is *this* the word, the one word, that precisely expresses our meaning, and the tone in which we want to express it?

Tone

I use the word *tone* here to mean the aspect of a piece of writing that a reader may perceive to give the impression of being such things as aggressive or emollient; condemnatory or exculpatory; didactic or receptive; elegant or ugly; emotive or neutral; frenetic or relaxed; manipulative or fair-minded; objective or subjective; passionate or calm; polite or coarse; or some combination of such characteristics. Tone in writing – which is not the same thing as personal style (see pp. 33 and 41 below) – derives from the writer's purpose and point of view; and it is largely – though not entirely, for rhetoric will also be involved – established by the words chosen to express them.

This can be seen most plainly in the emotive language that is in common use in the tabloid newspapers and their analogues in the broadcast media. For instance, the neutral adjective *undeveloped* may be changed for polemical reasons to *backward, callow, crude, primitive, raw, retarded,* or *uncivilised*; while on the other hand a single emotive word can be substituted for a number of related but different meanings, as when *blast* is used as a verb to mean *censure, criticise, deprecate, disapprove of, display anger towards, dispraise, humiliate, insult,* or *put down*. The tone of such emotive writing is aggressive, coarse, and manipulative.

This degree of distortion, which is intended to interpret a newspaper story for its readers and even to prevent them from taking a balanced view of it, has no place in SWE; but even a writer who seeks to achieve a tone of calm, fair-minded neutrality will find both that he or she constantly has to choose one word rather than another, which means choosing one shade of meaning rather than another; and that the quiet tone of his or her prose will be just as apparent, if not as objectionable, as is the blaring tone of tabloid prose.

So the first task for the writer of SWE is to choose his or her words with great care, to worry at them until he or she is sure that they are exactly right. The vocabulary, which should be as free of jargon as convenience and the circumstances allow, must be appropriate to the subject; this said, it must exploit the riches of the word-stock, seeking precise shades of meaning. Words should be chosen, moreover, to attract the reader by being varied, interesting, and comprehensible; while monotony can be avoided by the interplay of monosyllables with polysyllables, of the concrete with the abstract, of words of Germanic origin with those deriving from Romance languages. Writing attractive prose becomes more fluent with practice; but the writer should always remember that choosing the right, the precise, word is more important than choosing the pleasing one.

There are also traps to be avoided, besides the mistakes of definition, grammar, and usage mentioned in Part I. Excessively emotive words used in the media have already been mentioned; and it should be remembered that it is easy to offend individuals or groups of people by an insensitive choice of words. The uneducated, the stupid, the senile, the mad, the diseased, the deformed, the deaf, the blind, the lame, and members of some ethnic groups – and indeed all who are perceived to be in some way disadvantaged or different from the rest – these people, or those who speak for them, will in some circumstances take offence if they are called by a blunt descriptive term rather than by whatever euphemism is currently acceptable.[3] But it is equally wrong to use absurd 'politically correct' euphemisms such as *vertically*

---

3. Euphemisms themselves come to seem offensive in their turn, and are replaced by new euphemisms; thus *negro* becomes *coloured*, which becomes *black*, which is then capitalised as *Black* (or *Afro-American*, *Afro-Caribbean*, and so on). Major dictionaries generally include terms such as *nigger* (while marking them as 'offensive'); but neither the Penguin *Roget's Thesaurus* nor the spellcheck program on my word-processor admits the existence of the word *negro* (let alone *nigger*). However, the wheel appears to be coming full circle in the United States, where a number of mostly black critics are now writing about American 'Negro' (capitalised) art and culture.

challenged for *shorter than average*, or *heightism* for discrimination against short people.

3   SENTENCES AND PARAGRAPHS

Sentences

There are various ways of defining a 'sentence' grammatically in written English. Perhaps the simplest is to say that it is a group of words, normally terminated by a full stop, that contains at least a subject and a finite verb (or predicate, which says what happens to the subject). Thus *John laughed* is a sentence, but *John's laugh* is not. This simplest of sentences can be elaborated by saying, for instance, *handsome John laughed loudly*, where the adjective *handsome* describes John's appearance and the adverb *loudly* describes the volume of his laughing. Then there are sentences of the form subject–verb–object, as in *John kissed Mary*; which can be reversed, *Mary kissed John*; and to which adjectives and adverbs (or adjectival or adverbial phrases) can be added to elaborate the meaning: *pretty, demure Mary gently kissed the embarrassed but willing John*. But the noun-clause *John kissing Mary* – which includes the present participle of a verb as part of a subject – is not a sentence because it lacks a predicate saying what happens to John in this situation.

A 'compound sentence' is usually made up of two simple sentences linked by a conjunction: *John laughed, and Mary kissed him*; *John offered to kiss Mary, but she did not want him to*. A 'complex sentence' consists of a main sentence (simple or compound) containing, or adjacent to, one or more sub-sentences (or clauses): *John, who is as kind as he is handsome, saw that Mary, whom he knew to be shy, did not want him to kiss her*, where the main sentence is *John saw that Mary did not want him to kiss her*, and *who is as kind as he is handsome* and *whom he knew to be shy* are descriptive sub-sentences (in this case relative clauses).

So much for definitions. What the writer of SWE needs to keep in mind is not so much the grammatical description of what he or she is writing as the fact that a sentence is a unit of sense, and preferably a fairly simple one. It is possible to drag out a sentence with conjunctions and subordinate clauses to almost any length, but the reader loses his way in the maze and the writer's object is frustrated. We have already said, in connection with grammar, that what we write should always *sound right*; and we can now add to this the second great rule of good writing, which is to *keep it simple*. In fact the writer will do well to say, preferably out aloud, each sentence while writing or revising it, to hear with both inner and outer ear that its meaning is immediately comprehensible, that it is grammatically correct, and that it has no false notes.

Paragraphs

If sentences are small sense units, paragraphs should be large ones. When the subject changes, even if only by a little, a new paragraph is usually desirable. But even if there is little perceptible change in a subject that occupies many lines, paragraphing can still help readers by giving them a chance to take a mental breath before they move on. If you look at the previous sub-section you will see that I have divided what would otherwise be a long and dense single paragraph on the grammatical nature of sentences into two paragraphs, even though the change of subject is only between the simpler and more complex forms of sentence; and that then definitions are finished with, and a new subject – the handling of sentences – makes a new paragraph mandatory.

Paragraphs can be of virtually of any length; sometimes they consist of no more than a sentence (usually a long one); sometimes they run to several pages. But, since it is the reader's comprehension and convenience that the writer's paragraphs should serve, extremes of length should be avoided as far as possible, and paragraphs should be provided that not only divide the text into helpful units of sense, but also make comfortable units of reading time. A good length is about 200 words.

Larger units

A similar view may be taken of the larger units of structure, namely the sections, chapters, and parts of an article or book: they too are sense units, and they are there to help the reader, to make the purpose of the author's book or article both more comprehensible and easier to absorb. In descending order of difficulty – after words, sentences, and paragraphs – these larger units will probably give the author the least trouble to arrange, being the scaffolding, so to speak, which is erected first, and on which the main part of the writing is then built.

4   STYLE AND PERSONALITY

An author's style, as opposed to the tone in which a particular work is written, is his or her distinctive and personal manner of writing; and it can differ from writer to writer just as much as can their manner of thinking, of social behaviour, of speaking, or of dressing. This was my fourth proposition: that each person's prose style can be as individual and attractive – or unattractive – as any other facet of his or her personality. And, just as we usually want to impress people favourably with our personality, so we should make the effort to write in a style that accords with that impression.

An attractive prose style, one that seemed to express its author's personality best, might for instance be simple but sharply accurate in exposition, harmonious in its cadences, and wryly humorous where humour is appropriate. It would avoid inappropriate or offensive words, awkward phrasing, and embarrassing facetiousness.

So much is obvious, but there are traps here too: ambiguity, verbosity, excessive elegance, and overblown rhetoric.

Ambiguity

Ambiguities range from obvious errors such as *The police did their best to stop sleeping on the pavement*, and the gravestone *Erected to the Memory/of/John McFarlane/Drown'd in the Water of Leith/By a Few Affectionate Friends*; through less obvious puzzles such as *the shop sells old and valuable furniture* (one kind of furniture or two?); to ambiguity that results from uncertainty: *the ship sank in the bay, but the divers who looked for the treasure could not find it* (is it known whether it was the ship or the treasure that could not be found?). Once ambiguities are recognised they are usually easy to put right.

Verbosity

A writer, especially one who is under contract to a publisher, may think of a book as a container which has to be filled with so much writing; and someone who has been asked to write an article for a journal is even more likely to think of the job as involving the production of so many thousand words. But this is a way of thinking that must be ruthlessly rejected if work of the best quality is to result. There is a right length for whatever is to be written; if less is written the subject will not have been dealt with adequately; if more (which is the commoner fault), style will have been sacrificed to bulking out the book. The rule is to write accurately but sparingly; never to say more than is necessary for a complete, rigorously economical exposition of the subject.

To show how verbosity can double the length of what is written without altering its sense, these are the last, economical ninety-nine words of a passage from Trevor-Roper's *The Last Days of Hitler* (which is discussed on pp. 79–80 below):

> Hitler and Eva Braun shook hands with them all, and then returned to their suite. The others were dismissed, all but the high-priests and those few others whose services would be necessary. These waited in the passage. A single shot was heard. After an interval they entered the suite. Hitler was lying on the sofa, which was soaked with blood. He had shot himself through the mouth. Eva Braun was also on the sofa, also dead. A revolver was by her side, but she had not used it; she had swallowed poison. The time was half-past three.

This is the same passage expressed in language that is excessively wordy (204 words):

> Hitler and Eva Braun shook hands with all fifteen of them, and then retired, alone, to the privacy of their suite in the subterranean bunker. All of them, all but Bormann and Goebbels, and those who would have to help to deal with the results of the events that were to take place (who would have included Guensche and Linge), were told to go away. Those few whose place it was to stay waited, listening in the passage outside the suite. One shot – one only – was heard in the confined space of the bunker. After waiting in the passage for a further interval, they went into Hitler and Eva Braun's suite. Hitler was lying, prone, on the sofa, in a pool of his own blood, which was soaking into the sofa's fabric.

He had pointed the barrel of his pistol into his mouth and pulled the trigger. Eva Braun was likewise on the sofa, beside him. She too was dead, though not as a result of a gunshot wound. There was indeed a revolver lying by her side, but it was unused. Instead she had ingested poison, and had died as a result. By now it was half past three in the afternoon.

Elegance

Prose that is graceful in its choice and arrangement of words is pleasurable to read; but if an attempt at elegance is obvious it will detract from the pleasure. One snare is Fowler's 'elegant variation', where the writer tries too hard to avoid repetitions (see pp. 21–2 above); but the greater part of excessive elegance is the result of making too free with such figures of speech as far-fetched analogies, the use of quotations (especially from foreign languages), the omission of conjunctions, alliteration and jingles (words echoing each other in rhyme or metre), phrases that are obviously periphrastic (saying something in a roundabout way) or hyperbolical (exaggerated), and so on; which lead us into the territory of rhetoric. Here is the passage from Trevor-Roper rewritten in a style of excessive elegance:

In a gesture, part-bourgeois, part *de haut en bas*, Hitler and Eva Braun shook hands with all those who had kept faith with them, and then returned to their suite, now to be the scene of their final, apocalyptic exit. The faithful, all but the greatest of them and those who stood and waited to serve on this one last solemn occasion, were given leave to leave them. Those few waited, *ohne Hast*, outside in the bare passage. Silence. Then a single shot echoed through the bunker. They waited; there was no second shot; then dared at last – *mortui non mordent* – to enter the death chamber. The sight that met their eyes was of Hitler lying on the sofa, soaked in his life's blood, shot fatally through the mouth; with Fräulein Braun, beside him in death as in life, a revolver spurned by her side, overcome by a mortal draught. It was half past three – Adolf's and Eva's beloved tea-time. (159 words)

Rhetoric

For a writer, rhetoric – the art of persuasive speaking or writing – is an essential professional skill; but, as with excessive elegance, if the rhetorical effort is obvious to the reader it defeats its own purpose. The commonest faults are over-elaborate metaphors, multiple repetitions; rhetorical questions (questions not requiring an answer); the over-elaborate balancing of matching or antithetical sentences, clauses, or phrases; and the choice of inappropriately emotive words. Many of these characteristics appear in the following version of the same passage in a style of overblown rhetoric:

> One last handshake – O fatal farewell! – and Hitler and Eva Braun retired to their suite to ring down the final curtain on the terrible drama of their lives. Their fellow-actors took their exits, all but the great ones and the humble spear-carriers who would assist at their obsequies. Those few – those happy few? – waited off-stage in the passage until they heard their cue: a single shot. They entered the suite – you can see it, can't you, framed in the cramped proscenium arch of the bunker? – audience now to the tableau at the end of the last act. Tableau indeed! There lay *der Chef*, the King of his besieged castle, total gules as his blood drained out onto the sofa on which he lay, shot through the mouth – the mouth of the greatest actor of them all, whose mesmeric speeches had drawn millions to his disastrous cause. Queen Eva, no more than a poor player before this final scene, lay by his side, but her blood mingled not with his, for her revolver lay unused while she had found her quietus in the poisoned cup. The clock, fatal bellman, struck half past three. (192 words)

5   REVISION

Having vaulted all these hurdles and got something down on paper, the writer has one job left to do: revision, which is absolutely essential to the production of good work. Hardly anyone – professionals included – can get everything right in a first draft, and nearly all good writers put time and effort into revising their work. The first thing to do, each time writing begins, is to read through and correct what was written last time;

which has the additional advantage of getting oneself into the mood for the next stint. Then whole chapters or sections can be revised, and parts of them rewritten if necessary, as they are completed; and finally the work should be put away for as long as possible after it is finished – preferably for two or three months – and read again with a fresh eye. A final polishing may be enough at this point; but it sometimes happens that substantial parts of the book or article will demand to be rewritten, and in an extreme case it may seem best to write the whole thing out again, with concurrent revision. If it does, so be it: anything is worth sacrificing for the sake of quality.

Relatively minor faults, like spelling mistakes and bad grammar, repetitions, awkward phrasing, and ambiguities, will probably be dealt with in the earlier revisions. In later revisions larger themes such as construction, consistency, clarity of expression (which usually means simplicity), rhythm and pacing may be tackled. Perhaps most importantly, anything that does not contribute to the meaning and impact of the book should be cut. This means cutting not only unnecessary verbiage and words and phrases that are used too often, but also explanations of what should be self-evident, anything that is not strictly relevant to the work, such as the fascinating results of peripheral research, and anything that follows the ending of the main theme. Passages that the author thinks particularly fine, which are likely enough to be inessential, should also be considered for removal. Writers often have to scrap whole chapters that have not worked, and sometimes have to discard as much as a year's work on a book. Less often than superfluities, under-writing may be identified, which is when a passage is actually too short to do the job it is meant for, such as an explanation that needs to be expanded.

When all this is done, the book or article may not be a masterpiece, but it will be much better than it was before; and it will be ready to be passed on to the copy-editor, who will find many more things to correct and revise (see section 7 below).

6   LAYOUT AND THE TYPESCRIPT

Apart from letters, most documents, whether they be memoranda, reports, journal articles, or books, should be typed and presented in approximately the same way. The following are the main points to be observed:

(1) The document should be typed (or printed out) on one side only of sheets of medium-weight, white, A4 paper. The typing should be at least competent, and its appearance should not be spoiled by too many manuscript corrections and alterations; it is better to retype a heavily corrected page. The typewriter or printer ribbon should be replaced as soon as the page begins to look grey, and (if a typewriter is used) the carbon paper should be changed frequently; it is never worth being mean about paper, ribbons, and carbons.

(2) Lines should be double-spaced, with a margin of at least an inch all round the page. Paragraphs should be indented four or five character spaces, but there should not be a blank line between paragraphs unless there is to be a 'white line' (indicating a break in the text) on the printed page. There should be the same number of lines on each full page of the typescript. There is no need to align ('justify') the right-hand margin, even if the typewriter or word-processor will do it.

(3) Dialogue is usually found in fiction, but may occasionally occur in SWE. The usual convention is that a new paragraph is used for each new speaker. If this is done for dialogue between two people, it is theoretically possible for the reader to know who is speaking however many speeches there are, but after half a page of it readers are liable to lose track and to suffer the annoyance of having to go back to the beginning and note the alternation of the speeches to find out where the dialogue has got to. This can be avoided by putting in an occasional 'he said', 'I said', 'said John', and so on, at appropriate points. (Although the repetition of words would normally be avoided, 'said' is a neutral word in this context, and it can be used frequently; 'asked' and 'replied' are also fairly neutral words here, but 'he laughed', 'she gasped', and so on, are less neutral and may sound mannered if they are used more than once in a particular dialogue.)

(4) Each chapter or main section should begin on a new page.

(5) Notes, whether they are to appear as footnotes or are to be collected at the ends of chapters or at the end of the book, should be typed out separately from the main text.

(6) The pages should be numbered consecutively in the top right-hand corner from the beginning of the typescript to the end; and the total number of pages should be given at the head of the first page. The pages of each chapter or main section should not be numbered separately. It is a good idea to precede each page

number with an acronym which identifies the book (and, for PC users, which also identifies the file to which the page belongs). The last page of the book should be unambiguously marked as such.

(7) In addition to the cover sheet of a document submitted for publication – which gives the author's name and address, biographical notes, the number of pages in the typescript, and the number of words in the whole book or article – it is wise to write the author's name and address again on the first and last pages of the text.

(8) The pages should not be bound or otherwise fastened together, unless they are to be photocopied and circulated without further transcription. They should be put in a folder or a cardboard box (the sort that the typing paper comes in), tied round with string.

(9) If a typescript has to be resubmitted to another publisher or department, it may be freshened up by retyping or reprinting any pages – for instance the first and last pages – that have become creased or thumbed during the earlier submission.

(10) The author should never let a manuscript or typescript leave his or her hands without keeping a copy (easy enough now that photocopying machines are so widely available). It may be safe to send off the only hard copy from a word-processor, provided that backup disks have been made.

7   COPY-EDITING

Publishers know, even though new authors may not, that the final typescript or printout of a book received from an author will not in practice be ready to be printed and published exactly as it stands, and that there are several ways in which it will have to be checked and improved. The person who does the checking and improving is the copy-editor, who works as an intermediary between the author and all those whose job it is to turn the typescript into a book. This copy-editor, who may or may not be a full-time member of the publisher's staff, works in two ways: as corrector, and as reviser.

As corrector the copy-editor (1) ensures that the typescript is consistent in following the publisher's 'house style' (or the author's own style) in matters of spelling, punctuation, abbreviations, and so on, and is internally consistent in repetitions of such things as names and references; and (2) sees that it gives unambiguous instructions to the typesetter and printer, specifying sizes of type, grades of sub-headings, positioning of illustrations, and so on. To do this the copy-editor needs no more than a good professional grasp of how books are made and presented.

As reviser the copy-editor has a more delicate and difficult task, for he or she is responsible for checking (3) that the whole presentation of the book – both content and organisation – is consistent and satisfactory; and (4) that the meaning of the text, sentence by sentence, is properly expressed and is without errors, gaps, or contradictions. To do this well, and without either giving offence to the author or degrading the text in style or content, is obviously a trickier matter than making the technical corrections described first. How far should the copy-editor go in making or suggesting revisions? The short answer is, as far as necessary and no further; but if the copy-editor can establish a friendly and productive relationship with the author – by post and on the telephone, or nowadays by fax and e-mail too – then a real contribution to improving the book can be, and frequently is, made by collaboration between them.

Every piece of writing that goes through the process of publication, be it a novel or a technical work or a newspaper article, is copy-edited. This book that you are reading has been copy-edited. So, when we come to look at examples of SWE in Parts III and IV, it must be borne in mind that nearly all of them have been copy-edited to a greater or lesser extent before publication. This is not obvious – the individuality of their style and content has not been flattened out or obliterated by copy-editing – but we must accept that we are not reading their authors' prose raw and unchecked.

Part III
Four Stylists

The writers whose styles are analysed in this part of the book – the philosopher and political activist Bertrand Russell (1872–1970), the statesman and historian Winston Churchill (1874–1965), and the novelists Virginia Woolf (1882–1941) and Evelyn Waugh (1903–66) – are chosen not only for the outstanding qualities of their prose, but also because their writings have been absorbed into the language and are inescapable influences on the way we write now. They were at the height of their powers during the first half of the twentieth century, but their antiquity is unimportant in this context, for their various skills have remained unsurpassed, and we can learn from them as profitably as we can learn from any more recent stylist.

There were similarities as well as dissimilarities between them. Russell and Churchill were both preceptorial in that each was concerned to inform, to teach, and to put a point of view, though their aims, and the methods they used, were not at all the same. Virginia Woolf and Waugh, on the other hand, shared the novelist's purpose of creating works of art, but again they used very different techniques. For, as stylists, they change partners: Russell and Waugh wrote prose that tends towards elegance, simplicity, clarity, and objectivity; prose which has a timeless quality that is as current now as it was when they were writing it fifty and more years ago. The prose of Churchill and Virginia Woolf seems by contrast more subjective, emotional, flamboyant, and involved; more personal, perhaps, and to this extent more dated. This is not of course to say that Russell and Waugh were less involved in what they were saying, or were less eager to communicate it, than were Churchill and Virginia Woolf, but that they sought their ends by different means.

1   BERTRAND RUSSELL

Bertrand Russell's background was both Welsh and aristocratic. Both his parents died soon after he was born in Gwent in 1872, and he was brought up by his grandmother, the widow of Lord John Russell, the Liberal prime minister who became the first Earl Russell (Bertrand Russell himself succeeded as the third Earl Russell in 1931, but he preferred not to use the title). After a private education at home, he went up to Trinity College, Cambridge, where he graduated with first-class honours in mathematics and philosophy in 1894. The following year he married Alys Pearsall Smith, daughter of a Philadelphia Quaker family and sister of the writer Logan Pearsall Smith. Shortly after his marriage he was elected a prize Fellow of Trinity, and set out on a long career that was as notable for its academic excellence as it was for its wide-ranging, controversial notoriety.

Russell's academic speciality was mathematical logic, to which his most important contributions were his two great treatises *The Principles of Mathematics* (1903), arguing that mathematics could be derived from logic, and *Principia Mathematica* (1910–13, with Alfred North Whitehead), which presented his theory in a complete formal system. During the same period he was developing a philosophical 'theory of types' and 'theory of descriptions', but in philosophy he was soon overtaken by Ludwig Wittgenstein, who came to Trinity as his pupil in 1912.

From then on Russell's main interests, and means of livelihood, were controversial politics, education, journalism, and popular scholarship. In 1916 he was sacked from his lectureship at Trinity – he was no longer a Fellow – and in 1918 imprisoned for actively opposing the war; while from 1949 he became increasingly involved in the cause of nuclear disarmament, joining the Committee of 100 and being imprisoned again in 1961. Throughout his long life he produced a stream of articles and books, including several outstanding works of popular scholarship, such as *The Problems of Philosophy* (1912) and *A History of Western Philosophy* (1945). As an educationalist he set up a progressive school; and he taught and lectured in China, in the United States, and – finally – back in Cambridge, where he was re-elected to a Trinity Fellowship in 1944. His honours after the Second World War included the Order of Merit and the Nobel Prize for Literature.

Personally Russell was charming, lucid, humorous, and ruth-less. He was four times married – besides engaging in much incidental philandering – and he retained the power of his extraordinary mind until he died in Wales in 1970 at the age of 98, his last major work being the three volumes of his *Auto-biography* (1967–9).

Russell was better able than any other writer of his time to explain difficult concepts – in his case the concepts of philosophy – in language that was plain, unencumbered, and crystal clear. Indeed there is a purity about his best prose that seems to parallel the purity of the mathematics and the logic that were the subject of his early academic achievements. To illustrate this, one can take almost any paragraph from *The Problems of Philosophy*, a textbook of about 100 succinct pages that he wrote in 1911 (when he was 39) for a teach-yourself series called The Home University Library, which published it in 1912. It is an out-standingly successful popularisation of the subject; it is still in print; and it has not been superseded as an introduction to some of the fundamental questions of philosophy. Here for instance is the beginning of the chapter on 'Truth and Falsehood':

> Our knowledge of truths, unlike our knowledge of things, has an opposite, namely *error*. So far as things are con-cerned, we may know or not know them, but there is no positive state of mind which can be described as erroneous knowledge of things, so long, at any rate, as we confine ourselves to knowledge by acquaintance. Whatever we are acquainted with must be something; we may draw wrong inferences from our acquaintance, but the acquaintance itself cannot be deceptive. Thus there is no dualism as regards acquaintance. But as regards knowledge of truths, there is a dualism. We may believe what is false as well as what is true. We know that on very many subjects different people hold different and incompatible opinions: hence some beliefs must be erroneous. Since erroneous beliefs are often held just as strongly as true beliefs, it becomes a diffi-cult question how they are to be distinguished from true beliefs. How are we to know, in a given case, that our belief is not erroneous? This is a question of the very greatest difficulty, to which no completely satisfactory answer is possible. (*The Problems of Philosophy*, Oxford University Press 1980, p. 69)

Here Russell takes us through his argument with such clear economy that it could not be abridged or paraphrased in many fewer words than he uses himself. Besides this it is noticeable that he employs no similes or metaphors, and scarcely any words that have an underlying metaphorical content (*confine*, line 5, is a possible one). The sentences are well balanced, and not too long for easy comprehension; the vocabulary is simple and free of specialist jargon; and the only figure of speech is the repetition of the main point, *it becomes a difficult question how they are to be distinguished from true beliefs*, in the form of the rhetorical question: *How are we to know, in a given case, that our belief is not erroneous?* This is prose that has the perfection of Bach's keyboard works, or the games of the great chess masters.

Russell's politics were for the most part pacifist, but he made a brief exception soon after the Second World War, when the United States alone had atomic weapons but when it was obvious to Russell that the Russians, and then others, would have them within a few years. He supposed that a nuclear pre-emptive strike might then be expected, with catastrophic consequences, and that the only way of preventing one would be the establishment of an international government with a monopoly of armed forces. He recognised that many people hoped that the United Nations would be able to keep the peace, but he considered it to be a weak organisation, incapable of effective action unless it was radically reformed. People would argue for appeasement of the Soviet Union, a method already proved disastrous in the 1930s: 'I myself supported this policy on pacifist grounds, but I now hold that I was mistaken ... It is not by giving the appearance of cowardice or unworthy submission that the peace of the world can be secured.' He went on:

> In dealing with the Soviet Government, what is most needed is *definiteness*. The American and British governments should state what issues they consider vital, and on other issues they should allow Russia a free hand. Within this framework they should be as conciliatory as possible. They should make it clear that genuine international co-operation is what they most desire. But although peace should be their goal, they should not let it appear that they are for peace at any price. At a certain stage, when their plans for an international government are ripe, they should

offer them to the world, and enlist the greatest possible amount of support; I think they should offer them through the medium of the United Nations. If Russia acquiesced willingly, all would be well. If not, it would be necessary to bring pressure to bear, even to the extent of risking war, for in that case it is pretty certain that Russia would agree. If Russia does not agree to join in forming an international government, there will be war sooner or later; it is therefore wise to use any degree of pressure that may be necessary. But pressure should not be applied until every possible conciliatory approach has been tried and has failed. I have little doubt that such a policy, vigorously pursued, would in the end secure Russian acquiescence. ('The Atomic Bomb and the Prevention of War', *Polemic*, London, July/August 1946.)

This article caused quite a stir at the time, for it was recognised that by *any degree of pressure that may be necessary* Russell could only mean that the United States should as a last resort use atomic weapons against the Soviet Union – our very recent ally – to force it into international co-operation before it developed atomic weapons of its own; and Russell did not reprint it among the collections of his papers published later, after he had become involved with the CND and become more anti-American. As it turned out he was wrong: there was no nuclear war between the two superpowers before the collapse of the Soviet Union; but we can sympathise with his fear today, when there is the possibility of nuclear proliferation to such unreliable regimes as those of Iraq.

Again Russell, while being mealy-mouthed about saying outright that America might have to drop atomic bombs on the Russians, writes prose that is lucid and precisely argued, though his journalism lacks the rigorous perfection of his philosophy. There are indeed no metaphors, and no rhetorical questions or other figures; but there are several rather slack metaphorical words, such as *framework*, *goal*, *ripe*, and *pressure*.

Russell wrote his last major work, the three volumes of his autobiography, when he was well into his nineties, but it is by any standards a remarkable work of self-revelation, recounting thoughts and deeds that many autobiographers might have thought shameful and have omitted. But here Russell acted on his profound belief that truth should be served above all things; and he also managed to avoid much self-justification. Here he recounts his falling out of love with his first wife, Alys Pearsall Smith, after six years of marriage in 1901:

> I went out bicycling one afternoon, and suddenly, as I was riding along a country road, I realised that I no longer loved Alys. I had had no idea until this moment that my love for her was even lessening. The problem presented by this discovery was very grave. We had lived ever since our marriage in the closest possible intimacy. We always shared a bed, and neither of us ever had a separate dressing room. We talked over together everything that ever happened to either of us. She was five years older than I was, and I had been accustomed to regarding her as far more practical and far more full of worldly wisdom than myself, so that in many matters of daily life I left the initiative to her. I knew that she was still devoted to me. I had no wish to be unkind, but I believed in those days (what experience has taught me to think possibly open to doubt) that in intimate relations one should speak the truth. I did not see in any case how I could for any length of time successfully pretend to love her when I did not. (*Autobiography*, vol. I, Allen and Unwin, London 1967, pp. 147–8)

He says further on that he justified his attitude to her, as well as to himself, by criticisms of her character, expressing them with a self-righteousness that he later found repulsive. But it is characteristic of him that, although he acknowledges that what he did and said to Alys was wrong (though partly justified by her shortcomings) he does not express, or seem to feel, much more than technical sympathy for what she suffered, the best he can do being to say *I had no wish to be unkind*; and, later, *Meanwhile Alys was more unhappy than I was, and her unhappiness was a great part of the cause of my own.*

And this is where the perfection of his philosophical prose, which he continued to be able to write until the end, failed to work on a human level. As a piece of SWE there is nothing wrong with this last extract; it is as clear and precise as ever. But the reader's sympathies call out for something more, for an expression in words of the passionate emotions that this episode must have generated, for acknowledgement that what happened was not just a logical development of Russell's falling out of love but a disaster that wrenched real human hearts.

Although the last of these extracts was written more than half a century after the first, there is not much development to be found in the style of the writing. Russell's great intellect, and his command of the explanatory if not of the emotional use of the English language, remained with him all his life; and, in the end, it may be that the example of his use of plain English for explication will be among his most valuable legacies.

2   WINSTON CHURCHILL

Winston Churchill, a grandson of the seventh Duke of Marlborough, was born in 1874 at Blenheim, Vanbrugh's baroque palace that was well suited to the flamboyant style of the Churchills. Educated at Harrow, where his academic attainments were negligible, he proceeded to Sandhurst, and thence to a commission in the 4th Hussars in 1894. From then on his adventures and achievements were various, extraordinary, distinguished, and too well known for us to have to follow them here, beyond saying that he became successively a cavalryman on active service (1897–8), a war correspondent (1899–1900), a prisoner of war (escaped, 1900), a Member of Parliament of great oratorical powers (1900), Home Secretary (1910), First Lord of the Admiralty (1911), a fighting soldier again (1915), Minister of Munitions (1917), War Minister (1919), Chancellor of the Exchequer (1924), First Lord of the Admiralty again (1939), and Prime Minister (1940, 1951). In 1908 he married Clementine Hozier (who survived him), and he died, partially paralysed by a stroke, in 1965 at the age of 91. This, it might be thought, was a life full enough to satisfy anyone, but in addition to his public service Churchill was a journalist, writer, and historian of great fecundity, scope, and power; and it is with this other, literary life of his that we are concerned here.

Churchill's major works were *The River War* (2 vols, 1899), an account of the reconquest of the Sudan, in which he himself had taken part; *Savrola* (1900), his only novel; *Lord Randolph Churchill* (2 vols, 1906), a biography of his father; *The World Crisis* (5 vols, 1923–31), a history of the First World War; *My Early Life* (1930); *Marlborough* (4 vols, 1933–8), a biography of his great ancestor the first Duke; *Great Contemporaries*

(1937–8), a biographical miscellany; *The Second World War* (6 vols, 1948–54); and *A History of the English-speaking Peoples* (4 vols, 1956–8). This would be a large output for a writer who had nothing else to do, and it is a truly astonishing one for a public figure on Churchill's gigantic scale. Some of it was self-serving (especially his accounts of his own part in the two world wars), but Churchill loved writing and history for their own sakes, he hardly ever wrote badly or boringly, and he would surely have been a notable historian and biographer even if he had failed as a politician.

For a specimen of Churchill's early prose we may turn to *My Early Life* which, though published in 1930, contains an exciting account of his escape from a Boer prisoner-of-war camp that was originally written in 1900 and is quoted verbatim. Though he had planned to escape with two other officers, Churchill was the only one to get away, and his article tells of the escape itself, and of the first part of his journey of 300 miles to Delagoa Bay in Portuguese East Africa, when he walked alone and hitched a ride on a goods train through the enemy's country. (He could not write publicly in 1900 about the rest of his journey for fear of endangering the British miners who gave him crucial shelter and help.)

Here is the last paragraph of the original account of 1900, which ends just before the meeting with the miners:

> The elation and the excitement of the previous night had burnt away, and a chilling reaction followed. I was very hungry, for I had had no dinner before starting, and chocolate, though it sustains, does not satisfy. I had scarcely slept, but yet my heart beat so fiercely and I was so nervous and perplexed about the future that I could not rest. I thought of all the chances that lay against me; I dreaded and detested more than words can express the prospect of being caught and dragged back to Pretoria. I found no comfort in any of the philosophical ideas which some men parade in their hours of ease and strength and safety. They seemed only fair-weather friends. I realized with awful force that no exercise of my own feeble wit and strength could save me from my enemies, and that without the assistance of that High Power which interferes in the eternal sequence of causes and effects more often than we are always prone to

admit, I could never succeed. I prayed long and earnestly for help and guidance. My prayer, as it seems to me, was swiftly and wonderfully answered. (*My Early Life*, Macmillan 1930, ch. 21)

This is journalism – it was written originally for *The Morning Post*, the paper which employed Churchill as a war correspondent – with a touch of a boy's adventure story, but even here Churchill's characteristic tone and ornate, declamatory style has begun to appear. There are no fewer than eight doublets in less than 200 words: *elation and excitement, nervous and perplexed, dreaded and detested, wit and strength, causes and effects, long and earnestly, help and guidance, swiftly and wonderfully*, plus the triplet *ease and strength and safety*. Note also the jingling *chocolate, though it sustains, does not satisfy*; and the elaborate sentence beginning *I realized with awful force* ... which, while it has the lofty tone of a Sunday sermon, also suggests derivation from the balanced sentence-structures of the eighteenth century.

The military disaster of Gallipoli – the attempted invasion of the Dardanelles in 1915 which was intended to lead to the capture of Constantinople and the end of Turkish participation in the war – has often been blamed on Churchill, who was at the time First Lord of the Admiralty, the political head of the Navy. But, although Churchill bore considerable responsibility for promoting the attack – it was intended at first to be primarily a naval operation – he was not responsible for its disastrous conduct, which led inevitably to defeat and the only possible response: evacuation. However, his emotions were bound up in Gallipoli to such an extent that, even when he looked back on it after the war, he still found it hard to accept the decision of a general sent out from England to advise the government whether to continue the fight or to withdraw:

> On October 14 it was decided to recall Sir Ian Hamilton and to send out in his place General Monro, an officer who had already commanded an army in France and was deeply imbued with Western[1] ideas. He belonged to that school whose supreme conception of Great War strategy was 'killing Germans'. Anything that killed Germans was right.

1. 'Western' meaning those who believed that the war could only be won on the main front, in France, and not in 'side-shows' such as Gallipoli.

Anything that did not kill Germans was useless, even if it made other people kill them, or kill more of them, or terminate their power to kill us. To such minds the capture of Constantinople was an idle trophy, and the destruction of Turkey as a military factor, or the rallying of the Balkan States to the Allies, mere politics, which every military man should hold in proper scorn. The special outlook of General Monro was not known to the Cabinet. His instructions were moreover exclusively military. He was to express an opinion whether the Gallipoli Peninsula should be evacuated, or another attempt made to carry it; ... General Monro was an officer of swift decision. He came, he saw, he capitulated. He reached the Dardanelles on October 28; and already on the 29th he and his staff were discussing nothing but evacuation. (*The World Crisis: 1915*, Thornton Butterworth, London 1923, p. 489)

This extract from his history of the Great War is Churchill at his most oratorical; in fact he writes as if he is to deliver the passage as a fighting speech in the House of Commons. He derides Monro as an army commander contaminated by the slogging match in France, whose mind, void of strategical insight and political wisdom, was fixed on slaughter, and who – irresistible phrase – came, saw, and capitulated. To Monro, sneers Churchill, Constantinople was an *idle trophy*, the consequences of its capture *mere politics, which every military man should hold in proper scorn*; and he came to his craven decision to evacuate within a mere twenty-four hours of his arrival. In fact the decision was the only one to which a sane soldier could come, and it was to Monro's credit that he came to it quickly; yet Churchill implies that it was still possible to continue the fight and win it, even though he must know in his heart that it was not.

Churchill became Prime Minister in 1940 when the Germans were poised for the rout of France and, as they hoped, the invasion of England. With France out of the war, they had only to defeat the Royal Air Force to realise their hope, and it was the conflict between the Luftwaffe and the RAF, known as the Battle of Britain, that was the country's first, essential success in the war. Churchill oversaw it, and afterwards recorded its main features:

The German Air Force had been engaged to the utmost

limit in the Battle of France, and, like the German Navy after the Norway campaign, they required a period of weeks or months for recovery. This pause was convenient for us too, for all but three or four of our fighter squadrons had at one time or another been engaged in the Continental operations. Hitler could not conceive that Britain would not accept a peace offer after the collapse of France. Like Marshall Pétain, Weygand, and many of the French generals and politicians, he did not understand the separate, aloof resources of an Island State, and like these Frenchmen he misjudged our will-power. We had travelled a long way and learned a lot since Munich. During the month of June he had addressed himself to the new situation as it gradually dawned upon him, and meanwhile the German Air Force recuperated and redeployed for their next task. There could be no doubt what this would be. Either Hitler must invade and conquer England, or he must face an indefinite prolongation of the war, with all its incalculable hazards and complications. (*History of the Second World War*, vol. II, Cassell, London 1949, pp. 282–3)

This is Churchill's prose in its mature excellence: compelling, euphonious and full-bodied, without drawing attention to the taste and skill with which it is composed. There are no false notes: the argument is deployed with grand simplicity, without boasting but with some pride in *the separate, aloof resources of an Island State*, our *will-power*, and the fact that *we had travelled a long way and learned a lot since Munich*. Note the Churchillian doublets *separate, aloof*; *recuperated and redeployed*; *invade and conquer*; *hazards and complications*.

There is no doubt that it was the same man who wrote all three of these pieces – there is for instance the same fondness for doublets in the last piece as there was in the first – but here there is an equally obvious development in the style; from the breathless story-telling of the first extract, through the oratorical figures of the second, to the compelling assurance of the last. We cannot all write like Churchill; nor should we want to; but the effect of his writing and his speeches on the development of the written language in the twentieth century has been great and beneficial.

3   VIRGINIA WOOLF

Born in 1882 (as was James Joyce), Virginia Woolf was the younger daughter of Sir Leslie Stephen (1832–1904), who was a scholar, a critic, the first editor of the *Dictionary of National Biography*, and a principal member of the 'intellectual aristocracy'.[2] Her childhood, like much of the rest of her life, was interrupted by periods of great unhappiness; and she became subject to bouts of severe depression which verged on madness. Although her sexuality was uncertain, she married Leonard Woolf in 1912, the two of them being members of a group of friends that was associated with Bloomsbury in London. (The other members of the group were Virginia Woolf's elder sister Vanessa, Vanessa's husband Clive Bell, Roger Fry, Desmond McCarthy, E. M. Forster, Lytton Strachey, Maynard Keynes, Duncan Grant, and David Garnett – intellectual aristocrats every one.)

The marriage was, on the whole, a success, and it was surely Leonard's strong support that made it possible for her to hold herself together for long enough to write her nine novels and her many essays and reviews. It was also Leonard's careful husbandry that made a commercial success of the Hogarth Press which they founded in 1917, at first no more than a simple printing machine and a limited range of type in the basement of their London house, but eventually a substantial publishing business which contracted its output to other printers. In 1941, during a particularly severe depression when even Leonard's help was not enough, Virginia Woolf drowned herself – after several previous attempts at suicide, and, coincidentally again, in the year of Joyce's death – when she was 59.

Virginia Woolf could be both shy and outspoken, good-natured and cruel, brilliantly perceptive and naive. She had charm and charisma, but it was not safe to fall in love with her, for men or for women. Her love of language was intense, and she handled it in a very personal way, but yet with great precision; like Stephen Dedalus, she wielded a cold steel pen.

The nine novels began with *The Voyage Out* (1915), and included *Night and Day* (1919), *Jacob's Room* (1922), *Mrs*

2. The phrase comes from the article of the same name by Noël Annan in *Studies in Social History: A Tribute to G. M. Trevelyan*, ed. J. H. Plumb, London 1955.

Dalloway (1925), *To the Lighthouse* (1927), *The Waves* (1931), and her last novel *Between the Acts* (1941). She also gave two important feminist lectures which were published in 1929 as *A Room of One's Own*; and wrote, among numerous other essays, a further feminist tract attacking militarism, *Three Guineas* (1938).

Novels of the 1920s and 1930s – and especially Virginia Woolf's novels – tended to be built chiefly on character, dialogue, and interior monologue, but they generally included descriptive passages written in SWE as well. Virginia Woolf's first novel, *The Voyage Out*, which had been begun by 1908 and was finished by 1913 (but not published until 1915) after much rewriting and revision, was fairly traditional in form, with a third-person narrator, dialogue in direct speech, and no interior monologue (the Joycean revolution was not to have its full effect until the publication of *Ulysses* in 1922). Here is a passage in which the character St John Hirst (an attempt at a portrait of Lytton Strachey) is introduced:

> Downstairs all was empty and dark; but on the upper floor a light still burnt in the room where the boots had dropped so heavily above Miss Allan's head. Here was the gentleman who, a few hours previously, in the shade of the curtain, had seemed to consist entirely of legs. Deep in an armchair he was reading the third volume of Gibbon's *History of the Decline and Fall of Rome* by candle-light. As he read he knocked the ash automatically, now and again, from his cigarette and turned the page, while a whole procession of splendid sentences entered his capacious brow and went marching through his brain in order. It seemed likely that this process might continue for an hour or more, until the entire regiment had shifted its quarters, had not the door opened, and the young man, who was inclined to be stout, come in with large naked feet. (*The Voyage Out*, Duckworth, London 1915, ch. 9)

Although this is essentially a conventional way of introducing a new character in a novel, describing Hirst physically by a few noticeable appearances and mannerisms (*had seemed to consist entirely of legs; deep in an armchair; knocked the ash automatically, now and again, from his cigarette and turned the page; capacious brow*), the ironic humour and fantastic imagery of

Virginia Woolf's mature style is beginning to appear. Here she proposes the idea of Gibbon's elaborate sentences being a regiment of soldiers tramping, one by one, from the printed page to Hirst's brain. It is also characteristic of Virginia Woolf's tendency to being disorganised that she gets the title of Gibbon's book slightly wrong.

Next is a later piece of her prose fiction, this one from *To the Lighthouse* (1927), where the character of the philosopher Mr Ramsay is drawn from those aspects of her late father, Sir Leslie Stephen, which his children had most disliked (her fiction often took a biographical turn):

> Had there been an axe handy, a poker, or any weapon that would have gashed a hole in his father's breast and killed him, there and then, James would have seized it. Such were the extremes of emotion that Mr Ramsay excited in his children's breasts by his mere presence; standing, as now, lean as a knife, narrow as the blade of one, grinning sarcastically, not only with the pleasure of disillusioning his son and casting ridicule upon his wife, who was ten thousand times better in every way than he was (James thought), but also with some secret conceit at his own accuracy of judgement. What he said was true. It was always true. He was incapable of untruth; never tampered with a fact; never altered a disagreeable word to suit the pleasure or convenience of any mortal being, least of all his own children, who, sprung from his loins, should be aware from childhood that life is difficult; facts uncompromising; and the passage to that fabled land where our brightest hopes are extinguished, our frail barks founder in darkness (here Mr Ramsay would straighten his back and narrow his little blue eyes upon the horizon), one that needs, above all, courage, truth, and the power to endure. (*To the Lighthouse*, Hogarth Press, London 1927, ch. 1)

This is a more complex narrative than the previous extract, mixing the languages of thought and conversation with SWE. Starting with a sentence and a half of straight description, the narrator begins to mix objectivity with a subjective experience of James's thoughts, later bringing in reports of Mr Ramsay's own sermonising. It is not always clear who is speaking. Is *narrow as the blade of one* [sc. a knife] said by the narrator or thought by

James? Is *never tampered with a fact* the narrator speaking, or James, or is it a direct quotation from Mr Ramsay? And which bits of the syntactically enigmatic ending from *should be aware ... that ... the passage to that fabled land* to *courage, truth, and the power to endure*[3] belong to the narrator, to James, to Mr Ramsay – or even to some other member of the family? This sentence also contains an elaborate and contradictory metaphor, in which failure in *that fabled land* is strangely expressed in the language of hope and endurance.

The third extract is from Virginia Woolf's feminist and pacifist tract *Three Guineas* (1938), identifying men with militarism, and discussing women's attitudes towards war. Here she attributes the enthusiasm of the daughters of educated men for war in 1914 to their 'private house' education which reinforced their dependence on a status quo supported by empire and war, but from which they longed to escape; and which she would remedy by supporting women's higher education and the opportunities for influence and power for women that would result from it:

> But her unconscious influence was even more strongly perhaps in favour of war. How else can we explain that amazing outburst in August 1914, when the daughters of educated men who had been educated thus rushed into hospitals, some still attended by their maids, drove lorries, worked in fields and munition factories, and used all their immense stores of charm, of sympathy, to persuade young men that to fight was heroic, and that the wounded in battle deserved all her care and all her praise? The reason lies in that same education. So profound was her unconscious loathing for the education of the private house with its cruelty, its poverty, its hypocrisy, its immorality, its inanity that she would undertake any task however menial, exercise any fascination however fatal, that enabled her to escape. Thus consciously she desired 'our splendid empire'; unconsciously she desired our splendid war. (*Three Guineas*, Hogarth Press, London 1938, penultimate paragraph of I)

Whatever we think of it, Virginia Woolf's opinion of the matter is sincerely held and passionately argued; and *Three*

---

3. The syntactical puzzle is solved by adding '[is]' before *one that needs, above all, courage, truth, and the power to endure.*

Guineas aroused answering passions on both sides of the question, from women as well as from men, when it was originally published and for long afterwards. As usual she makes her polemic very personal, though equally characteristically the prose remains precise, smooth and well balanced. She draws the reader into the discussion (*how else can we explain*) in a huge rhetorical question that follows the well-brought-up young women as they rushed to their various sorts of war work, where they persuaded young men that it was heroic to fight – did many young men really need to be persuaded of this in 1914? – and that war wounds deserved not only their care but their praise as well. The catalogue of war works is followed by a catalogue of the iniquities of *the education of the private house*, to escape which, she argues, young women were led to support the war, unaware of why they were doing it. She ends with a splendid rhetorical flourish, balancing *our splendid empire* with *our splendid war*. Soon after *Three Guineas* was written the Second World War began, and women again flocked into war work and the services, first as volunteers and then as conscripts; but this time there was less to escape from, and little talk of the heroism of fighting.

The development of Virginia Woolf's fictional style from *The Voyage Out* to *To the Lighthouse* is plain enough: in the earlier novel she was writing in the Edwardian style of E. M. Forster, in the later one she had read the modernists and become a modernist herself. The last extract, being polemical, is in a different style again, though still connected with the second one by the passion of its argument.

4   EVELYN WAUGH

Evelyn Waugh was born in 1903 into a family that was placed somewhere in the middle of middle-class England. His father Arthur was a 'literary' man, a genial belletrist and employee of a publishing house, who was not quite a member of the intellectual aristocracy, but who was able to send his younger son to a minor public school (Lancing) and a minor Oxford College (Hertford). At Oxford, where he learned to drink a lot and mixed with Etonians and men from the smarter colleges, Waugh found his dream – a dream not of academic but of social success among the upper classes. Unhappily for him it was a dream unrealised, for he was unalterably middle-class, speaking to the end of his life with an 'ow' diphthong that revealed his North London origins; and, more importantly, because he was a great literary artist, with the artist's sense of isolation, and the artist's destructive ability to recognise the moral poverty and neglected intellect that might lie behind smart, charming, and beautiful exteriors.

After doing badly in his exams at Oxford in 1925, Waugh taught for a couple of years at a private school; he was married unsuccessfully to Evelyn Gardner in 1928 (she left him and they were divorced the following year); and then, in 1930, he was received into the Roman Catholic Church – the most important event in his life, as he was to see it – which gave him the emotional and intellectual security that he knew he needed. This sense of security was enhanced when he married Laura Herbert, the daughter of a Catholic convert, in 1937, and they proceeded to bring up seven children. He died, an alcoholic, after Mass on Easter Sunday 1966, sitting on the lavatory – an irony that he would certainly have appreciated; he was 63.

Personally, Waugh had his faults. He was often drunk and he took too many sleeping pills. He frequently neglected his family. He could be as childishly selfish and as savagely rude as he could be charming and funny; and he was especially unpleasant in his demeaning treatment of those he considered to be his inferiors, such as the men he commanded during the war, and even his own children. But all this was no doubt the price he, and others, paid for his genius as a novelist; for, like him or loathe him, it is fair to say that no other English novelist of the first half of the twentieth century surpassed him for craftsmanship and style, and that few equalled the unsparing insights of his best work.

Although he remained a devoted Catholic, and although he was to write about Catholicism, Waugh was not just a 'Catholic novelist'. The Waugh who wrote the first, hilarious, and ferocious satires *Decline and Fall* (1928) and *Vile Bodies* (1930) is recognisably the same Waugh who wrote *Scoop* (1938), *Put Out More Flags* (1942), *The Loved One* (1949), and *Men at Arms* (1952). There were other Waughs as well: the one who wrote the nostalgic and hugely successful *Brideshead Revisited* (1945) and the one who wrote the extraordinary, self-revelatory *The Ordeal of Gilbert Pinfold* (1958).

The texts of Waugh's early novels consisted largely of dialogue, but there was some good, plain prose as well. Here is a paragraph from *Vile Bodies* (1930), which introduced one of his great comic characters, Lottie Crump (based on Rosa Lewis of the Cavendish Hotel, who had been associated with Edward VII when he was Prince of Wales, and other grandees):

> Lottie Crump, proprietress of Shepheard's Hotel, Dover Street, attended invariably by two Cairn terriers, is a happy reminder to us that the splendours of the Edwardian era were not entirely confined to Lady Anchorage or Mrs Blackwater. She is a fine figure of a woman, singularly unscathed by any sort of misfortune and superbly oblivious of those changes in the social order which agitate the more observant *grandes dames* of her period. When the war broke out she took down the signed photograph of the Kaiser and, with some solemnity, hung it in the menservants' lavatory; it was her one combative action; since then she has had her worries – income tax forms and drink restrictions and young men whose fathers she used to know, who give her bad cheques, but these have been soon forgotten; one can go to 'Shepheard's' parched with modernity any day, if Lottie likes one's face, and still draw up, cool and uncontaminated, great, healing draughts from the well of Edwardian certainty. (*Vile Bodies*, Chapman and Hall, London 1930, ch. 3)

This paragraph in SWE from an early novel does not yet have all the smooth assurance that Waugh was to achieve later on, but it is still a very competent and engaging beginning to a chapter. Waugh's narrator chooses a number of precisely apt words which help to give the extract its tone of cool irony: *singularly unscathed, agitate, with some solemnity, combative, parched with modernity, healing draughts*; and the metaphor of the well of Edwardian certainty in the last sentence (from *one can go to ...*) brings the paragraph to a richly satisfying conclusion. The narrator uses the historic present tense to draw the reader into the story, slipping into the past tense only the for sentence concerning the removal of the Kaiser's portrait. At the end of that sentence (*it was her one combative action;*) the rhythm would have been improved by the substitution of a full stop for the semicolon, since the following sentence changes both subject and tense.

Brideshead Revisited (1945) is narrated in the first person, but the *Sword of Honour* trilogy (1952–61) has a third-person narrator attached for the most part to the point of view of Guy Crouchback, the chief character, and it is representative of Waugh's mature style. This second extract is taken from near the beginning of the first volume:

> The Crouchback family, until quite lately rich and numerous, was now much reduced. Guy was the youngest of them and it seemed likely he would be the last. His mother was dead, his father over seventy. There had been four children. Angela, the eldest; then Gervase, who went straight from Downside into the Irish Guards and was picked off by a sniper his first day in France, instantly, fresh and clean and unwearied, as he followed the duckboard across the mud, carrying his blackthorn stick, on his way to report to company headquarters. Ivo was only a year older than Guy but they were never friends. Ivo was always odd. He grew much odder and finally, when he was twenty-six, disappeared from home. For months there was no news of him. Then he was found barricaded alone in a lodging in Cricklewood where he was starving himself to death. He was carried out emaciated and delirious and died a few days later stark mad. That was in 1931. Ivo's death sometimes seemed to Guy a horrible caricature of his own life, which at just that time was plunged in disaster. (*Men at Arms*, Chapman and Hall, London 1952, ch. 2)

Now Waugh's prose has become simpler; there are no metaphors or other figures of speech, and the sad irony of this family's history – of Gervase's death in France, of Ivo's madness – is in the story and the sentence-structure, rather than in the choice of word and phrase. The one long sentence describing Gervase's death ends with a tail of four adjectival clauses (from *fresh and clean and unwearied*) describing his condition and exactly what he was doing when he was shot, which draw out its pathos; while the description of Ivo's decline and death is given in a series of five stark, relatively short sentences (from *Ivo was always odd*), which speak not so much of the pathos as of the horror of his madness, evoking the 'horrible caricature' of Guy's own life.

In 1953, poisoned by repeated overdoses of bromide and chloral which he took without his doctor's knowledge as sleeping draughts, Waugh set off by himself on a ship bound for the Far East, in the hope that the voyage would cure him. On this ship he had a series of terrifying hallucinations which caused him to believe that he was being spied on and persecuted by some of the other passengers. Later he told the whole story of his experiences in one of his last novels, *The Ordeal of Gilbert Pinfold* (1957), a work in which he directed his novelist's eye upon himself in a feat of ruthless self-description. Here is the central paragraph of the narrator's description of Mr Pinfold:

> His strongest tastes were negative. He abhorred plastics, Picasso, sunbathing, and jazz – everything in fact that had happened in his own lifetime. The tiny kindling of charity which came to him through his religion sufficed only to temper his disgust and change it to boredom. There was a phrase in the thirties: 'It is later than you think', which was designed to cause uneasiness. It was never later than Mr Pinfold thought. At intervals during the day and night he would look at his watch and learn always with disappointment how little of his life was past, how much there was still ahead of him. He wished no one ill, but he looked at the world *sub specie aeternitatis* and he found it flat as a map; except when, rather often, personal annoyance intruded. Then he would come tumbling from his exalted point of observation. Shocked by a bad bottle of wine, an impertinent stranger, or a fault in syntax, his mind like a cinema camera trucked furiously forward to confront the offending object close-up with glaring lens; with the eyes of a drill sergeant inspecting an awkward squad, bulging with wrath that was half facetious, and with half-simulated incredulity; like a drill sergeant he was absurd to many but to some rather formidable. (*The Ordeal of Gilbert Pinfold*, Chapman and Hall, London 1957, ch. 1)

No one has written a better description than this of the way Waugh presented himself to many of his acquaintances. It is deeply comic, and to achieve his effect Waugh has used, not the flat, repressed style of Guy Crouchback's narrator in *Men at Arms*, but the more full-blooded language of his earlier novels. He begins gently with the understated irony of *the tiny kindling of charity*; *designed to cause uneasiness*; *except when, rather often, personal annoyance intruded*. But this turns out to be the introduction to the astonishing, long last sentence beginning *Shocked by a bad bottle of wine ...*, in which Waugh, fallen from his 'exalted' point of observation and losing his temper, describes first his outraged mind and then his furious advancing glare with the metaphor of a film-camera lens that 'trucks' (the usual word is 'tracks') in to become the eyes of a drill sergeant, bulging *with wrath that was half facetious, and with half-simulated incredulity ... absurd to many but to some rather formidable.*

The differences between these examples of Waugh's prose demonstrate not so much its development as his skill in adapting his style to the subject and tone of his fiction. His very first novel, *Decline and Fall* (1928), published when he was 25, was extraordinarily accomplished; and, like Churchill, he rarely wrote a bad or boring line thereafter.

As well as demonstrating the skill and flair of these four stylists, and reminding us of the great influence that they have had on later writers, these extracts from their work also show that each one had a distinct and personal style. So distinct were their styles, indeed, that they are immediately recognisable, not only in their authors' formal writings, but also in their informal writings such as personal letters.

Part IV
Case Studies in Style and Method

Most of the following extracts are in SWE, and most of them are from texts that are intended to convey information in a more or less serious way. They are divided into the following genres, or particular types of writing: autobiography, biography, business and institutional documents, (descriptive) fiction, history, journalism, language, literary criticism, philosophy, sociology and psychology, religion, technology and computing, and science. It will be seen that, although each genre tends to have its own tone (about which something is said in the headnotes), the basic style does not differ much between those that use SWE. There are other genres which are not normally composed in SWE, such as poetry, drama, fictional dialogue, private letters, diaries, informal memoranda, and electronic communication, and which are not included here.

Most of the extracts are of recent origin but, although SWE, like every other form of language, develops over time, writers of SWE may not develop with it, so that an older writer may use a slightly older form of the language than a younger one.[1]

1 AUTOBIOGRAPHY

An autobiography is an account of someone's life written by the subject. As with all historical accounts, autobiographies cannot include everything that has happened, and autobiographers are obliged to select some things for inclusion and to leave others out; and they use this process of selection to produce accounts that will conform to the manners of their time, and also to

1. See the examples of writing over considerable periods of time by four stylists in Part III, above.

explain and justify certain parts of their lives. For this reason an autobiography is normally less reliable about some aspects of the subject's life than a biography written by someone else; but, uniquely, an autobiography can include, at its author's discretion, things about the subject that cannot be known to anyone else.

Autobiographies are commonly written – as are the three examples here – in SWE, but some come close to being fiction and are written in semi-fictional form, with dialogue given in direct speech. Fiction itself is also used sometimes by novelists as a disguised form of autobiography, in such first-person novels as Dickens's *David Copperfield* (1850) and Christopher Isherwood's *Mr Norris Changes Trains* (1935), and in the meta-fictional asides in John Fowles's *The French Lieutenant's Woman* (1969; see pp. 74–5 below).

Captain Eden at the capture of the Messines Ridge, 1917

We found few enemy survivors among their forward positions, but it was at this early stage that I came upon the only fatal casualty I witnessed among our riflemen that day. The man had just fallen and lay spread-eagled on the ground, mortally wounded and already unconscious. I knew the rifleman for one of our most trusted soldiers and, for some reason I cannot explain, I was overwhelmed for the moment with the most bitter sadness. Perhaps it was the helpless position in which his body lay, the sudden and pathetic waste of a young life, a boy determined to do his duty. It all seemed so miserably unfair. Quite possibly he had been hit by a fragment of our own barrage, but that altered nothing. He had done what he set out to do and by his firm will he had helped to save many lives, for which he paid with his own. The momentary flash of that scene is still fresh in my mind. (Anthony Eden, *Another World: 1897– 1917*, Allen Lane, London 1976, pp. 158–9)

In this memoir of his service in the First World War, written in his old age some sixty years after the event, Eden uses extremely simple prose to bridge the gap back to the young infantry officer who experienced this death in 1916–17, with stock phrases appropriate to the period: *mortally wounded; one of our most trusted soldiers; most bitter sadness; pathetic waste; determined to do his duty; by his firm will he had helped to save many lives, for which he paid with his own.* The flash of sadness – especially bitter because it came at one of the few times in that war when a British attack by massed infantry succeeded in reaching all its planned objectives – is lived again in all its naive poignancy, written as if by a 20-year-old in 1917.

A trilingual polymath recalls a transcendental experience

One day during the summer holidays, in 1919, I was lying on my back under a blue sky on a hill slope in Buda. My eyes were filled with the unbroken, unending, transparent, complacent, saturated blue above me, and I felt a mystic elation – one of those states of spontaneous illumination which are so frequent in childhood and become rarer and rarer as the years wear on. In the middle of this beatitude, the paradox of spatial infinity suddenly pierced my brain as if it had been stung by a wasp. You could shoot a super-arrow into the blue with a super-force which could carry it beyond the pull of the earth's gravity, past the moon, past the sun's attraction – and what then? It would traverse inter-stellar space, pass other suns, other galaxies, Milky Ways, Honeyed Ways, Acid Ways – and what then? It would go on and on, past the spiral nebulae, and more galaxies and more spiral nebulae, and there would be nothing to stop it, no limit and no end, in space or time – and the worst of it was that all this was not fantasy but literally true. (Arthur Koestler, *Arrow in the Blue*, Hamish Hamilton, London 1952, pp. 51–2)

Evidently Koestler wrote this key passage of his autobiography with an excitement that bubbles through the prose, insisting that his readers share it with him. The rhetorical piling-up of adjectives and nouns, the repetitions, the hurrying from dash to dash, and the sudden halt at the end, all convey the immediacy and importance that the revelation had for him both when it happened and when he recollected it over thirty years later.

The word 'beatitude', blessedness, is a surprising but apt choice for describing a transcendental experience. 'Acid Ways' might suggest hallucinogenic drugs to the modern reader, but in fact the *OED*'s earliest date for 'acid = LSD' is 1966. Koestler's first language was Hungarian, his second German, and only his third English, but since 1940 all his books had been written in

English, and here he handles the language with great accomplishment.

Emotion recollected, not in tranquillity

You must imagine conversations like this taking place every evening, in kitchens and sitting-rooms all over Germany. Painful encounters, truth-telling, friendship-demolishing, life-haunting. Hundreds, thousands of such encounters, as the awful power of knowledge is slowly passed down from the Stasi to the employees of the Gauck Authority, and from the employees of the Gauck Authority to individuals like me. Who then hold the lives of other people in our hands, in a way that most of us would never otherwise do.

Might it not, after all, be wiser to allow them their own particular imaginative mixture of memory and forgetting, of self-respect built on self-deception? Or is it better to confront them? Better not just for yourself, for your own need to know, but for them too? Even in her first confused reaction, 'Michaela' herself said 'really it's good that you've shown me this'. (Timothy Garton Ash, *The File: A Personal History*, HarperCollins, London 1997, p. 105)

These two paragraphs come at the beginning of a sub-section recalling Garton Ash's investigation of the file kept on him by the secret police of East Germany, when he went back after the collapse of the DDR to confront the informers and secret policemen who had contributed to it. He writes in a style of rhetorical intimacy, buttonholing the reader in order to say something that is of great importance to him, investing the writing with hints of intimate informality. The second sentence has no main verb; the last sentence of the first paragraph is separated from its predecessor not by the expected comma but by a full stop, which forces the reader to pause; and the three questions in the second paragraph are not merely rhetorical, but are asking the reader to try to find his or her own answers to them. This is writing of an intensity that both exposes the author and relieves him of some of his torment.

It is very different from Koestler's uninhibited narrative, which is also of great importance to the author but employs a different sort of rhetoric: where Koestler holds forth, sharing his excitement with anyone who will listen to him, Garton Ash speaks softly, one to one, with deep emotion.

2   BIOGRAPHY

Biography, the account of a person's life written by someone else, has a history going back to classical times, but modern English biography involving a frank appraisal of the subject's character and doings written in SWE, based on considerable research and with the presentation of relevant documentary evidence, begins with Boswell's unparalleled *Life of Samuel Johnson* (1791). But, however frank the biographer may intend to be, and however he or she is constrained by the nature and availability of the evidence, decisions will still have to be made about what is to be included and what not, and also about what attitude is to be taken towards the subject; for, while the biographer may intend to occupy a position of neutrality, there is likely to be a tendency towards sympathy with the subject or the lack of it, towards approval or disapproval. In the examples which follow, the first is markedly tendentious in denigrating the subject; the second is much more objective, and friendly rather than unfriendly; while the third tells a story in semi-fictional style that is, if anything, to the discredit of the subject.

Lytton Strachey attacks Cardinal Manning

When Manning joined the Church of Rome he acted under the combined impulse of the two dominating forces in his nature. His preoccupation with the supernatural might, alone, have been satisfied within the fold of the Anglican communion; and so might his preoccupation with himself: the one might have found vent in the elaborations of High Church ritual, and the other in the activities of a bishopric. But the two together could not be quieted so easily. The Church of England is a commodious institution; she is very anxious to please; but, somehow or other, she has never managed to supply a happy home to superstitious egotists. (Lytton Strachey, *Eminent Victorians*, 'Cardinal Manning', section 5, Collins, London 1918)

Strachey set out, from the position of a Bloomsbury intellectual who had never achieved very much himself, to destroy the reputations of four Victorians who had, in one way or another, achieved a good deal: Manning, Florence Nightingale, Dr Arnold, and General Gordon. Ignoring, or denigrating, his subjects' strengths, he concentrated on their weaknesses; and, using elegant, balanced phrases, he abused and ridiculed them in a way that is as immediately beguiling as it is in the long run recognised as false. (Of Florence Nightingale: *There was humour in her face; but the curious watcher might wonder whether it was humour of a very pleasant kind.*) The combination of a debunking tone with a style that is attractively polished has influenced later writers, but they have rarely equalled Strachey in venom.[2]

Here Strachey attacks the reputation of Henry Manning (1808–92), an eloquent preacher and Anglican High Churchman who went over to Rome in 1851, and became Catholic Archbishop of Westminster in 1865. He was no saint, but he was not a bad man, and to the end of his life he was tirelessly active in benevolent organisations and in the temperance movement; but Strachey is determined to show him as motivated only by egotistical self-interest and a ludicrous belief in the spiritual value of ecclesiastical ritual, *the two dominating forces in his nature*. It is a commonplace that we are most irritated by those faults in others of which we are ourselves guilty; and there was, perhaps, a good deal of what he saw wrong with Cardinal Manning in Strachey himself, an egotistical intellectual involved in the social rituals of Bloomsbury.

Gladstone and the Parnellite victory of 1885

This overwhelming expression of Irish opinion made a profound impression upon Gladstone. It did not strike him like a thunderclap when the results came out because the anticipation of such a development had affected his thinking at least since the early autumn. But expectation was one thing and the reality of counted votes another, and the clarity with which the Irish constituencies had spoken was unmistakable. The solidity was such as to create a fear that virtually all the Irish MPs from the three southern and western provinces together with a sizeable minority from

2. Strachey's equally well-written literary criticism, however, was both less offensive and more convincing, as in his classic *Landmarks in French Literature*, 1912.

Ulster might withdraw from Westminster and set up their own assembly in Dublin. (Roy Jenkins, *Gladstone*, corrected edn, Macmillan, London 1996, p. 535)

Politicians make the best biographers of other politicians because they know from experience what the life is like, where ambition must be checked and where it can be indulged, where to stand firm and where to compromise. Lord Jenkins is a master of the form, producing political biography at its best and SWE at its most urbane. He is as skilled a writer and scholar as he was a Minister of the Crown. Each word in this sympathetic life of the greatest Liberal leader is well chosen, each sentence is carefully crafted; perhaps in this extract *together with a sizeable minority from Ulster* could have been enclosed with commas, but then perhaps I am too fond of them.

Lord Jenkins has also written a fascinating political autobiography, *A Life at the Centre* (1991), which has the virtues of his political biographies without risking the exposure of his private life.

Tolstoy one up on Turgenev

Turgenev got back from abroad in May 1861, and almost immediately invited Tolstoy to stay at his estate of Spasskoye. The meeting was happy enough, and there was a good dinner. After the meal Turgenev proudly produced the newly completed manuscript of his novel *Fathers and Children* and, placing his friend on the drawing-room sofa, put the masterpiece into Tolstoy's hands. Then he left his guest to savour the experience of reading it alone.

When Turgenev returned to the drawing room to see what impression the novel was making upon Tolstoy, he was disconcerted to see the young man stretched out on the sofa, fast asleep. Since both the participants in this marvellous scene were novelists, that is to say falsifiers, it is hard to know how much of it actually took place, and how much was a fiction of their own brains. Tolstoy improves the story by saying that he opened his eyes and was just able to see Turgenev's back slinking through the door of the room, and trying not to be noticed. (A. N. Wilson, *Tolstoy*, Hamish Hamilton, London 1988, p. 171)

This pleasing anecdote occurs in A. N. Wilson's excellent biography of Tolstoy, and it fairly represents the style of the whole: pungently and sometimes loosely written, with an informal, novelish flavour which is appropriate to the author, who is himself an accomplished novelist, as well as to his great subject. The irony of the joke is of course that *Fathers and Children* really was a masterpiece, so that Turgenev's embarrassed fishing for praise was not unreasonable; while Tolstoy's snub showed up his own entirely unreasonable jealousy of a fellow artist.

The story is told conversationally, with a rather rambling second sentence in the second paragraph, as if among friends after dinner.

3   BUSINESS AND INSTITUTIONAL DOCUMENTS

No business or institution can operate without a considerable flow of documents, which enable it to perform its work and to record the results. They fall into five main categories.

(1) *Internal memos and instructions* are frequently informal, and may exist in electronic form alone, or in hard copy, or in both.

(2) *External correspondence*, usually more formal in style than the internal documents, is generally similar to private correspondence, and is sent out in hard copy.

(3) *Minutes of meetings* can range from brief notes to extensive summaries of what was said and decided, kept by a 'secretary' who, in larger organisations, may be a senior permanent official. They usually begin with introductory statements (heading; date, place, and time; the names of those present; apologies for absence; minutes of the last meeting; and so on); and proceed to record the doings of the meeting in a series of separate, numbered paragraphs. Minutes are vital records which will be needed for future reference; they are normally written in SWE and kept in hard copy.

(4) *Reports and presentations* are analogous to articles in professional journals and features in newspapers. They may be written in continuous SWE, or be split up into headed, and sometimes numbered, sections and paragraphs. They are usually circulated in hard copy.

(5) *Assessments and references concerning personnel* have some of the characteristics of biography; they are written in SWE, and sent out or filed in hard copy.

Documents in the last three categories are usually composed in SWE. They can be very well written – especially in universities and government departments – but (as in the examples given here) they can also be woolly, careless, or insincere. These examples are taken from real documents, with names suppressed.

An Extract from the Minutes of a University Council

CO.96/186. *Financial recovery of the university, 1996–2000* … The present meeting of the Council was in the Vice-Chancellor's view an important stage in the financial recovery of the university which had begun in October 1995 and continued ever since. The Vice-Chancellor indicated his increasing confidence in the underlying strategy and the willingness of all sectors of the university to accept that there was little choice and that the current planning process would take the university into a more secure future. Everyone must however recognise that there was some distance to travel, and financial and managerial vigilance could not be relaxed. He drew attention to the inevitable element of repetition of information at each stage, necessary because the process was a continuing one and exhaustive in its non-stop pressures on senior administrators and academic managers. Thus the revised strategy was to take steps to pull away from the current financial difficulties as soon as possible, and to release the enormous potential for future growth.

This third-person narrative actually says very little, but says it dully and at length. No doubt the Vice-Chancellor's remarks, which look as if they were made for the record (for waffling of this sort could hardly encourage anyone into action), were equally boring. The whole paragraph is characterised by tired phrasing: *the current planning process would take the university into a more secure future; everyone however must realise that there was some distance to travel; vigilance could not be relaxed;* and *the process was a continuing one and exhaustive* [or was it 'exhausting'?] *in its non-stop pressures on senior administrators and academic managers.*

An organisation for penal reform argues in favour of voting rights for prisoners

1.8   Those who support the enfranchisement of prisoners believe it would encourage them to take more responsibility for their lives, and help them prepare for release. Prisoners would become aware of the principles and processes of British democracy and of their rights and responsibilities as citizens. Instead of being exiled from society they would see themselves as part of, not apart from, the wider community.

1.9   Second, granting the vote to prisoners would encourage politicians to take more of an active interest in prisons, which in turn would raise the level of the debate about future penal policy.

1.10   Third, the loss of voting rights for prisoners is something of a lottery. Regional variation in sentencing mean [*sic*] it is frequently where you live and not the offence, which determines sentence and hence the loss of voting rights. ...

1.12   The argument raised against voting rights for convicted prisoners at the TUC was that the public would object to violent offenders being granted the vote. However, this is not a principled objection. Moreover, prisons are not full of violent offenders. ...

1.14   It is a fundamental aim of the Prison Service to prepare prisoners for release. Voting rights would help build a sense of responsibility amongst prisoners and make them feel more a part of society. Popular democracy should not stop at the prison gate.

It is taken for granted in this document that convicted prisoners should be treated as members of society, and not excluded from it. It may be that prisoners' reformation would be advanced by their inclusion in society, but the case is not argued. Only one objection to their inclusion is mentioned: *that the public would object to violent offenders being granted the vote* (1.12), which is said to be 'not principled' – presumably meaning that it is a practical, not a theoretical, objection – and which is illogically considered to be irrelevant because *prisons are not full of violent offenders*. Note also in the same section that *The argument raised against voting rights for convicted prisoners at the TUC was that* ... is comically ambiguous. The presentation is written in acceptable SWE, but its short, rather crude sentences may draw attention to the lack of rigour in its argument.

Beware the Greeks when they send references

Mr X, who came to this company as Records Clerk five years ago, was educated at Y School. He then took a Higher National Diploma in Accounting, and worked for eighteen months as a junior clerk with Messrs Z and Co. Since coming to us, Mr X has worked conscientiously in all the major Divisions of the firm, and is well known to all his colleagues for his tireless efforts on behalf of the Staff Club. He wants to make a move now to the senior position you are advertising as he is about to be married.

Mr X's record of attendance here has been exemplary, with only two days sick leave during the whole five years that he has been with us. He has moreover proved himself to be entirely trustworthy and honest in handling client accounts and petty cash. As you will see when you interview him, Mr X dresses smartly, and can hold his own in conversation.

The key to this carefully-written reference is to be found in what it does not say, rather than in what it does. Mr X may indeed work conscientiously and regularly, help out at the Staff Club, deal honestly with money, and be of good appearance. What the referee does not say is whether he is good at his work, whether his colleagues like him, and whether the firm regrets the prospect of losing him. In fact Mr X's work, though conscientious, is slow and inaccurate, he is a tiresome bore, and the firm would be glad to see him move on. Perhaps the prospective employer should ring up the referee, who, while he avoided writing the whole truth, might tell it if challenged directly.[3]

---

3. Some years ago a major university employed as Librarian a man who, in his previous post, was known to be an alcoholic; this had not been apparent to the appointments committee at the interview, and no one had enquired privately whether anything important had been omitted from the written reference.

4 FICTION

We use the term 'fiction' – an invented or imaginary thing – for stories that are made up for the entertainment, instruction, and aesthetic pleasure of their audience; and fiction in this sense is, and has been for three centuries, the dominant literary form: novels, novellas, and short stories reproduced in books and periodicals for a wide variety of readers. Novelists do use SWE, but for them it is usually subsidiary to other forms of writing, especially dialogue (recorded in direct and reported speech), and since the 1920s interior monologue, which are frequently preferred to plain SWE both for telling the story and for the development of fiction's central ingredient, character.[4]

Writing fiction in SWE

Bad weather, other odd jobs, mere lack of energy, had all contributed to allowing the unlit bonfire, projected as a few hours' clearing and burning, to become an untidy pile of miscellaneous débris; laurel (cut down months before), briars, nettles, leaves, unsold rubbish from a jumble sale, on top of it all several quite large branches of oak and copper beech snapped off by the gales. In spite of fog, something calm, peaceful, communicative, about the afternoon suggested the time had come to end this too long survival. A livid sky could mean snow. That dense muffled feeling pervaded the air. The day was not cold for the season, but an autumnal spell of mild weather – short, though notably warm that year – was now over. It had given place to a continuous wind blowing from the west, dropped the night before, after bringing down a lot of leaves and the sizeable boughs. (Anthony Powell, *Hearing Secret Harmonies*, Heinemann, London 1975, p. 243)

This atmospheric beginning of a chapter near the end of the last volume of Anthony Powell's great *roman fleuve*,[5] *A Dance*

---

4. See also the SWE in examples of the fiction of Virginia Woolf and Evelyn Waugh in Part III, above.
5. A *roman fleuve*, literally a 'river novel', is a sequence of novels which traces the fortunes of its characters over a period of time, such as Trollope's Barchester novels and his political novels, Proust's *A la recherche du temps perdu*, and C. P. Snow's *Strangers and Brothers*.

to the Music of Time, is written in straightforward SWE, clear, simple, and unencumbered with metaphors or other figures of speech. It has a slight colloquial flavour, as is appropriate for the first-person narrator of the novel, but it is based firmly on the standard written form.

Writing fiction on autopilot

And perhaps even among the klondikers there might have been one or two of these [sc. crooks] – men who had seen a way of enriching themselves; a dangerous way perhaps, but what of that? When so many were dipping their hands into the pot and coming up with gold, why should not they? Every man for himself was surely the order of the day. And though the icy port of Murmansk might not have appeared the most likely of places for stumbling on the means of making a quick killing, appearances could be deceptive.

It was, however, a well known fact that even the best laid of schemes had a habit of going disastrously wrong. You might make yourself as rich as Croesus, but you could end up by losing everything, including your life. That was the way of the world. (From a thriller of the 1990s)

These are the last two paragraphs of the opening section of a thriller. The prose sounds tired, which is perhaps not surprising since this is the author's *ninety-first* book. Perhaps he was trying to follow the (Russian) crooks' train of thought here, but the narrative reads as if it was written automatically. Metaphors change (the pot from which gold is dipped becomes *a quick killing*, both being clichés), in a bog of weary phrases (*what of that?*, *every man for himself*, *appearances could be deceptive*, *best laid of schemes*, *disastrously wrong*, *rich as Croesus*, *the way of the world*). There has been no effort made here to find the right word, the telling phrase, the effort which raises prose from boring predictability and gives it individuality and life.

The author breaks the mould

I do not know. This story I am telling is all imagination. These characters I create never existed outside my own mind. If I have pretended until now to know my characters' minds and innermost thoughts, it is because I am writing in (just as I have assumed some of the vocabulary and 'voice' of) a convention universally accepted at the time of my story: that the novelist stands next to God. He may not know all, yet he tries to pretend that he does. But I live in the age of Alain Robbe-Grillet and Roland Barthes: if this is a novel, it cannot be a novel in the modern sense of the word. (John Fowles, *The French Lieutenant's Woman*, Cape, London 1969, ch. 13)

'Metafiction' is the technical term for fiction that is about itself; and here, in perhaps the finest metafictional novel of recent times, Fowles breaks the mould of the omniscient narrator in his pastiche mid-nineteenth-century novel; and he speaks to the reader in his own person, as he has done already and is to continue to do in a series of asides, commenting on the story from the perspective of the mid-twentieth century. The first sentence of this extract from the beginning of a chapter answers the narrator's question at the end of the preceding chapter: 'Out of what shadows does she come?'; and for a couple of pages more Fowles continues to address the reader directly in his own voice, which becomes increasingly conversational, about the nature of fiction.

In fact the author breaks the mould so thoroughly here that, out of context, the passage reads more like a mixture of auto-biography and literary criticism than fiction; and yet it is not so. The metafictional asides of *The French Lieutenant's Woman* are an integral part of the whole fictional structure, and are readily accepted as such by the reader.

5   HISTORY

History – meaning here records of past events in human societies – has classical antecedents in the works of historians such as Herodotus, Thucydides, Julius Caesar, and Tacitus, who, like their successors down the ages, might choose to write broadly or narrowly, engaging in anything from sweeping histories of the whole world throughout recorded time to limited accounts of particular people or events in particular places. Nowadays some historical work is still broadly based (there are recent inclusive histories, for instance, of Europe and of the United States), and some is very narrow indeed, involving a great deal of research to produce a small nugget of useful – or occasionally useless – information. But, whatever their scope, historians writing today nearly always use SWE, differences in their language resulting chiefly from their degree of specialisation and therefore from the special vocabulary that they employ.

Serious history that is easy to read

Formally speaking, the war came as though King George V[1] still possessed undiminished the prerogatives of Henry VIII. At 10.30 p.m. on 4 August 1914 the King held a privy council at Buckingham Palace, which was attended only by one minister[2] and two court officials. This council sanctioned the proclamation of a state of war with Germany from 11 p.m.[3] That was all.[4]

1. George V (1865–1936), second son of Edward VII: married Princess Mary of Teck, 1893; king, 1910–36; changed name of royal family from Saxe-Coburg to Windsor, 1917; his trousers were creased at the sides, not front and back.
2. Lord Beauchamp, first commissioner of works, who succeeded Morley as lord president of the council on the following day.
3. Why 11 p.m.? It is impossible to say. The ultimatum to Germany demanded an answer *here* (i.e. London) by midnight. After its dispatch someone unknown recollected that German time was an hour in advance of Greenwich mean time, and it was decided that the ultimatum should expire according to the time in Berlin. Why? Perhaps for fear that the German government might give a favourable, or equivocal, answer; perhaps to get things settled and to be able to go to bed; probably for no reason at all.
4. War was declared against Austria-Hungary on 10 August.

(A. J. P. Taylor, *English History 1914–1945*, Pelican edn 1973, pp. 26–7)

The spare style of Taylor's main narrative is enlivened by a commentary of entertaining but nevertheless serious and informative footnotes. In the first footnote the apparently irrelevant information about the creasing of the King's trousers suggests that he belonged to another age; in the second the lack of political involvement in the declaration of war is emphasised by the sole presence at the council of an otherwise forgotten minister; while the third footnote implies that some of the people concerned wanted to get the declaration over with for discreditable or even trivial reasons. This is surely an effective way of writing history, showing that events happen on several levels, and that there is more than one way of approaching them. The prose of the main narrative is admirably simple and clear; the biographical footnotes, such as footnote 1 here, are given in abbreviated form, but the explanatory notes are written in an unabbreviated prose that is more informal than that of the main text.[6]

It is interesting to compare Taylor's account with the entry in the King's diary for the same day, which records his reactions to what had happened in words that have a moving and even child-like simplicity:

> Tuesday August 4th. I held a Council at 10.45 to declare war with Germany. It is a terrible catastrophe, but it is not our fault. An enormous crowd collected outside the Palace; we went on the balcony both before & after dinner. When they heard that war had been declared, the excitement increased & May & I with David went on to the balcony; the cheering was terrific. Please God it may soon be over & that he will protect dear Bertie's life. Bed at 12.0. (Quoted in Harold Nicolson, *King George the Fifth: His Life and Reign*, Constable, London 1952, ch. 15, section 4)

Two historians record Lenin's last illness, 1922–3

Lenin returned to work later that month, and in the two months of lucidity left to him, in the brief intervals when

6. Taylor's footnotes could be minor masterpieces. Here is one from the original edition of the same book (cut from the Pelican edition): 'The inhabitants of Scotland now call themselves "Scots" and their affairs "Scottish". They are entitled to do so. The English word for both is "Scotch", just as we call les français the French and Deutschland Germany. Being English, I use it' (*English History 1914–1945*, Oxford University Press 1965, p. 5).

permitted to work, dictated short essays in which he gave expression to a desperate concern over the direction Soviet policy had taken during his illness and charted the course of reforms. These essays are distinguished by lack of cohesion, a digressive style, and repetitiveness, all symptoms of a deteriorating mind. The most damaging of them remained unpublished in the Soviet Union until after Stalin's death. Initially used by Stalin's successors to discredit him, later, in the 1980s, they served to legitimize Mikhail Gorbachev's *perestroika*. The writings dealt with economic planning, cooperatives, the reorganisation of Worker-Peasant Inspection, and the relationship between the party and the state. Through all his later writings and speeches runs, as a common theme, the sense of despair over Russia's cultural backwardness: he now came to regard its low level of culture as the principal obstacle to the construction of socialism in Russia. (Richard Pipes, *Russia under the Bolshevik Regime*, HarperCollins, London 1994, p. 475)

Taken from the third volume of Richard Pipes's scholarly history of Russia before, during, and after the Bolshevik revolution, this is a good example of plain academic SWE. It is clear, to the point, rather dry, and without any attempt at inappropriate elegance. There is one unobtrusive metaphor in *he gave expression to a desperate concern over the direction Soviet policy had taken during his illness and charted the course of reforms*; and the choice of words and phrases is precise and telling. Pipes's prose serves its purpose – to say, simply, what happened – very well indeed; and there is no way of telling that his first language was not English but Polish – or that his current dialect is AmE rather than BrE.

Here now is another historian writing about Lenin's decline in a similarly broad treatment of the same period of Russian history:

These fragmentary notes, which later became known as Lenin's Testament, were dictated in brief spells – some of them by telephone to a stenographer who sat in the next room with a pair of headphones – between 23 December and 4 January. Lenin ordered them to be kept in the strictest secrecy, placing them in sealed envelopes to be opened only by himself or Krupskaya. But his senior secretaries were also spies for Stalin and they showed the notes to him. Throughout these last writings there is an overwhelming sense of despair at the way the revolution had turned out. Lenin's frenzied style, his hyperbole and obsessive repetition, betray a mind that was not just deteriorating through paralysis but was also tortured – perhaps by the realization that the single goal on which it had been fixed for the past four decades had now turned out a monstrous mistake. Throughout these last writings Lenin was haunted by Russia's cultural backwardness. (Orlando Figes, *A People's Tragedy: The Russian Revolution 1891–1924*, Cape, London 1996, pp. 797–8)

Orlando Figes, a younger English historian, begins here by writing about Lenin's notes attacking Stalin (Pipes's 'the most damaging of them'), and then goes on to discuss all the writings of Lenin's last two months. His prose is looser, livelier, and more familiar than Pipes's, and his details help to bring Lenin's haunted last days to life: the stenographer with headphones in the next room, the sealed envelopes, the spies sneaking off to Stalin; all leading up to the appalling *realization that the single goal on which it* [Lenin's mind] *had been fixed for the past four decades had now turned out a monstrous mistake.* There is also the unstated dramatic irony that we know, as Lenin did not, that it was a mistake that was to be further compounded by Stalin, and that the whole edifice was to come crashing down seventy years later.

When Figes's book was published, Pipes complained that Figes had copied some of his material; but convergence is inevitable when two historians tell the same story using the same sources, as when Pipes speaks here of Lenin's 'sense of despair over Russia's cultural backwardness', and Figes says that 'Lenin was haunted by Russia's cultural backwardness'. Figes must indeed have been informed and influenced to some extent by Pipes's previous work – he would be an incompetent historian if he had not been – but this is not the same thing as plagiarism.

The death of Hitler investigated

Meanwhile Hitler had finished lunch, and his guests had been dismissed. For a time he remained behind; then he emerged from his suite, accompanied by Eva Braun, and another farewell ceremony took place. Bormann and Goebbels were there, with Burgdorf, Krebs, Hewel, Naumann, Voss, Rattenhuber, Hoegl, Guensche, Linge, and the four women, Frau Christian, Frau Junge, Fraeulein Krueger, and Fraeulein Manzialy. Frau Goebbels was not present; unnerved by the approaching death of her children, she remained all day in her own room. Hitler and Eva Braun shook hands with them all, and then returned to their suite. The others were dismissed, all but the high-priests and those few others whose services would be necessary. These waited in the passage. A single shot was heard. After an interval they entered the suite. Hitler was lying on the sofa, which was soaked with blood. He had shot himself through the mouth. Eva Braun was also on the sofa, also dead. A revolver was by her side, but she had not used it; she had swallowed poison. The time was half-past three. (H. R. Trevor-Roper, *The Last Days of Hitler*, first published 1947, 4th edn, Macmillan, London 1971, p. 220)

The brilliant result of interrogations carried out by a young historian who was a German-speaking intelligence officer in the immediate aftermath of the war in Europe in 1945, *The Last Days of Hitler* is a classic of history written immediately after the events it describes. It is a definitive work that could only have been researched and written in 1945–6, when the survivors (such as some of those named in this paragraph) were still alive and their memories still fresh; and it has the immediacy of oral history controlled by the discipline of the professional historian.

The prose is both simple and economical.[7] The effect of authenticity is intensified by Trevor-Roper's dead-pan, unemotional reporting; and no word is wasted in the whole paragraph, the sentences falling neatly into place. The only word that is not in the style of simple reporting is 'high-priests', referring to Bormann and Goebbels as the keepers of the faith in Hitler's court.

---

7. Just how simple and economical is demonstrated on pp. 34–6 above, where a part of Trevor-Roper's paragraph is rewritten in other, less satisfactory, styles.

6 JOURNALISM

It has already been shown (pp. 29–30 above) how language can be perverted in the baser forms of tabloid 'journalese', the purpose of which is to manipulate as much as to inform the reader. But there is a higher journalism, that of the broadsheet newspapers and more intellectual news magazines, which use SWE with skill and good taste, and which for the most part avoid the clichés, the excessive use of nouns to qualify other nouns, the inappropriate choice of words – because they are short, or emotive, or fashionable, or punning – that both discredit and popularise the tabloids. (Even the broadsheets now include features and special sections that are written in styles other than SWE to appeal to special groups of their readers, such as those interested in sports, fashion, travel, food, and so on; and to particular age groups.)

Between these extremes come a wide range of weekly and monthly journals and magazines aimed at readers with special interests, which are written in an equally wide range of styles, but in most cases using special vocabularies appropriate to their subjects. They include numerous periodicals for women, teenagers, homemakers, countrymen, farmers, gardeners, beekeepers; and enthusiasts for sports of all kinds, various sorts of music, science, science fiction, the paranormal, cars, motorbikes, racing, DIY, keeping fit, and so on.

On the introduction of a Bill of Rights

Britain's government is about to fulfil an election promise by saying precisely how it will incorporate the European Convention on Human Rights into British Law. Properly done, incorporation could launch a much-needed legal revolution in Britain, one of the few established democracies where even basic civil liberties, such as the freedoms of speech and assembly or the right to a fair trial, do not enjoy special legal protection. Properly done, incorporation could also lead directly to fulfilment of the most important of all Labour's constitutional pledges: enactment of a British bill of rights. Unfortunately, the government has no intention of handling this properly.

Government sources have indicated that there will be no question of infringing the sovereignty of Parliament in any

way. British judges will be told to interpret British laws so
that they comply with the convention. But the Law Lords,
Britain's supreme court, will not be given the power to
knock down those acts of Parliament which cannot, even
by the most convoluted interpretation, be made to comply
with the convention. (*The Economist*, London 25 October
1997, fourth leader 'Fudging British Rights', pp. 19–20)

The firm, rather prim, schoolmasterly tone of *The Economist*
is in evidence at the beginning of this leader, which tells the
government off for behaving improperly by not proposing to give
the European convention unlimited supremacy over British Acts
of Parliament. Also in evidence is the precision of the argument
and the spare clarity of the prose, characteristics which are rarely
equalled and never regularly surpassed in British journalism
today. There are no extended metaphors and few metaphorical
phrases (*knock down those acts* is the chief example); but there
is an effective rhetorical build-up from *Properly done* repeated at
the beginning of the second and third sentences to *the government has no intention of handling this properly* at the end of the
first paragraph.

The Times, as will be seen in the following extract, takes the
opposite position, and supports the ultimate law-making power
of Parliament:

As the Government's White Paper says, interpretations
of the convention have evolved down the years to reflect
'changing social attitudes'. In Britain, framing laws to
protect rights in the light of social evolution has always
been a matter for Parliament. That process, whatever its
detractors, has been a democratic guarantor of liberty.

However true it may be that the convention reflects the
spirit of Magna Carta, the fact remains that such generality
is at odds with the detailed, case law-based practices of
British justice. The justification for incorporation could
only be that it enlarged the freedoms of the citizen under
the law. But some articles in the convention could be
interpreted in such a way as to restrict them instead. The
question, who decides, is therefore of paramount importance.

Hence the second, equally serious reservation, which is

that incorporation could erode divisions established down the centuries between Parliament's legislative supremacy and the strictly interpretative function of the judiciary. (*The Times*, London 25 October 1997, first leader 'The Bill for Rights', p. 23)

Although of a high standard, the prose here lacks the incisiveness of *The Economist*'s parallel leader, and has a fruitier tone that makes slightly heavy reading. It includes a few tired phrases (*in the light of, However true it may be … the fact remains, reflects the spirit of, is at odds with, paramount importance*) and awkward constructions (*case law-based practices; The question, who decides, is therefore …*). However, there can be no doubt about what is meant; and in fairness it must be remembered that, while *The Economist* has the leisure of being a weekly, *The Times* has to produce new leaders every day.

The world's oldest cave paintings

Journalists around the world went into a frenzy in January last year when French cave researcher Jean-Marie Chauvet unveiled a remarkable collection of prehistoric rock art. Chauvet and his friends had discovered the paintings just a few weeks earlier in a cavern at Vallon-Pont-d'Arc in southern Ardèche. Some 300 paintings and at least as many engravings depict about a dozen species of animal, several never before seen in rock art. The paintings are made of ochre, charcoal and haematite.

In their clamour to understand the importance of the find, the reporters turned their spotlight on rock art expert Jean Clottes, an archeologist with the Ministry of Culture. How old were the paintings? And who could have created such exquisite works of art?

At that time the pigment had not been radiocarbon dated, so Clottes relied on his long experience of studying cave art to estimate the age of Chauvet's find. Based on the style of the graceful animals in the pictures, he told journalists they were probably between 18 000 and 20 000 years old.

He was way off the mark. A few months later, to his amazement, carbon dating put some of the paintings at 31 000 years old, making them the oldest in the world.

(*New Scientist*, London 13 July 1996, 'Stone Age Picassos',
p. 33)

Here, in contrast to *The Times* and *The Economist*, the weekly
New Scientist uses a modified version of the breathless style of
popular journalism, with an inappropriate headline (*Stone Age
Picassos*), short paragraphs, short exclamatory sentences, omission of the definite article before people's titles, direct questions,
hyperbolical phrases (*went into a frenzy, way off the mark*), and
a mixed and hackneyed metaphor (*In their clamour to understand the importance of the find, reporters turned their spotlight
on rock art expert Jean Clottes*). It is not that the prose is unclear
or the story uninteresting. The objection to the use of journalese
of this sort to tell an important story with honest intent is that it
tends to trivialise the subject by recalling the manipulative style
of the less scrupulous tabloids.

A Consumerist Airhead Addresses the Young

Call me a consumerist airhead if you like, but if I were
on holiday in LA I wouldn't pass up the opportunity of
sashaying round some upmarket shopping mall in search
of – shame on me! – designer clothing. OK, my eyes would
soon glaze over (if only to shield themselves from those
dazzling, super-buffed marble floors and megawatt chand-
eliers), and I'd be reduced to a zombie. In fact just the kind
of zombie our cover star Jewel – seasoned singer of deep
and meaningful folk songs – would cross the street to avoid.
The annoying thing about her anti-materialistic stance is
that you can't accuse her of hypocrisy. Having sold six
million copies of her album 'Pieces Of You' in America,
Jewel's laughing all the way to the bank, but she's not
shrieking 'Spend, spend, spend!' and buying up every scarf,
hat and boot in those oh-so-high-street stores Gucci and
Prada as if there was no tomorrow. (*The Times*, London 18
October 1997, *1015* section, 'Dominic Says', p. [2])

The colloquial, even more breathless style of this passage from
the section of *The Times* aimed at their pre- and early-teenage
readers would be at home in the more demotic tabloids. It is of
course manipulative, effectively recommending a way of life that
most of its intended readers cannot, and perhaps should not,

aspire to; the readers may well be able to see this for themselves, however, in which case it does not matter.

There is no need to point out examples of the hyperbolical vocabulary or the fashionable phrases, for they are omnipresent; but it is worth pointing out that, while it is not SWE, there is nothing wrong with the syntax of this passage, and that the paper's young readers could do worse than to take it as an example of how to write, using a more formal choice of words and phrases.

7 LANGUAGE

Most writing about language can be assigned to one of three large groups: writing about usage (how a language is used); about linguistics (the nature and structure of language); and about the history, genealogy, development, and interrelationships of languages. All three groups are usually expressed in SWE, though linguists are liable to use special vocabularies, and historians of the genealogy, and so on, of languages have to quote foreign words and phrases. The following extracts come from each of the three groups.

Eight manuals of usage consider mutuality

1864: What is '*mutual*'? Much the same as '*reciprocal*'. It describes that which passes from each to each of two persons ... And *mutual* ought never to be used, unless the reciprocity exists. (Henry Alford, *The Queen's English*, 1864, quoted in *The New Fowler's Modern English Usage*, 3rd edn, ed. R. W. Burchfield, Oxford University Press 1996, p. 509)

1871: ... *mutual* for *common*, an error not infrequent now even among educated people ... (Richard Grant White, *Words and their Uses*, 1871, quoted in *New Fowler*, p. 509)

1906: Every one knows by now that *our mutual friend*[8] is a solecism. *Mutual* implies an action or relation between

8. The widespread use of the phrase *our mutual friend* resulted from the popularity of Dickens's novel of 1865, though Dickens himself knew that it was a solecism, putting it in the mouth of the amiable but uneducated Mr Boffin.

two or more persons or things. (H. W. and F. G. Fowler, *The King's English*, 1906, quoted in *New Fowler*, p. 509)

1926: **mutual** is a well-known trap. The essence of its meaning is that it involves the relation, *x* is or does to *y* as *y* to *x*; & not the relation *x* is or does to *z* as *y* to *z*. (H. W. Fowler, *A Dictionary of Modern English Usage*, Oxford University Press 1926, p. 368)

1942, 1965: **mutual** = 'reciprocal' ... this being the safest sense in which to use it; ... and 'pertaining to both parties; common; in common' ... certainly a usage to be avoided. (Eric Partridge, *Usage and Abusage*, first published 1942, revised edn, Hamish Hamilton, London 1965, p. 194)

1948, 1954: *Mutual* in the sense of *common*, pertaining to both parties, as in *Our Mutual Friend*, goes back to the sixteenth century, according to the *OED*, but is 'now regarded as incorrect'. Perhaps the reason why it is so difficult to restrain the word to its 'correct' meaning is the ambiguity of *common*. 'Our common friend' might be taken as a reflection on the friend's manners or birth. On the other hand it would be a great pity if *mutual* became so popular in its 'incorrect' sense that we could no longer rely on it when we need it for its correct one. (Sir Ernest Gowers, *The Complete Plain Words*, 2nd edn, Pelican 1973 [from *Plain Words*, HMSO 1948], p. 45)

1983, 1993: **mutual** (1) Felt, done, etc., by each to(wards) the other ... (2) Standing in a (specified) relation to each other, e.g. *Kings and subjects, mutual foes* (Shelley). This sense is now rare. (3) Common to two (or more) parties, e.g. *a mutual friend* or *acquaintance*. Sense (3) is acceptable in a small number of collocations, such as the two indicated, in which *common* might be ambiguous. (E. S. C. Weiner and Andrew Delahunty, *The Oxford Guide to English Usage*, Oxford University Press, 2nd edn 1993, pp. 150–1)

1996: The contest between the two main meanings of the word remains unresolved, but one can say with reasonable certainty: (*a*) *Mutual* used to mean 'reciprocal' is, of course, acceptable ... (*b*) So too are phrases of the type *a mutual friend, a mutual acquaintance*, in which *common* might be ambiguous, implying vulgarity ... (*c*) *Mutual* is also acceptable in many other sentences with the meaning 'pertaining to both parties': e.g. *of mutual benefit to both the Scots and the English* ... (*d*) But if it is possible idiomatically to use *common* or *in common* (in constructions of type (*c*)) this should be done: e.g. *They could discuss problems they had in common.* (*The New Fowler's Modern English Usage*, 3rd edn, ed. R. W. Burchfield, Oxford University Press 1996, p. 509)

What is notable about these extracts – apart from the move from the complete prohibition to the permission, in some circumstances, of *mutual = common* – is the correct, economical English of their authors; which is indeed what we should expect. The use of SWE here does not appear to change much from 1864 to 1996, though of course the earlier extracts are very short. Most of them in fact are markedly similar to each other, with the exception of Fowler's neat 'algebraic' formulation of 1926.

A linguist on the nature of grammar

The principle underlying grammar is unusual in the natural world. A grammar is an example of a 'discrete combinatorial system'. A finite number of discrete elements (in this case, words) are sampled, combined, and permuted to create larger structures (in this case, sentences) with properties that are quite distinct from those of their elements. For example, the meaning of *Man bites dog* is different from the meaning of any of the three words inside it, and different from the meaning of the same words combined in the reverse order. In a discrete combinatorial system like language, there can be an unlimited number of completely distinct combinations with an infinite range of properties. (Stephen Pinker, *The Language Instinct: The New Science of Language and Mind*, Penguin 1994, p. 84)

Here a professional in the science of linguistics explains the fundamental principle of grammar in a way that non-specialists can understand, provided that they know the meanings of the semi-technical words *finite* and *discrete*. The SWE is basic and plain which, ironically, is not always the case with linguistics. Pinker uses only one technical term (*discrete combinatorial system*), which he explains and illustrates; and he then goes on to point out that any one of us can make up at will a virtually infinite number of different sentences from the words at our command. It is a sobering thought; but, presented in Pinker's somewhat clinical prose, we accept it as one of the innumerable wonders of natural science.

Early English absorbs foreign words

It is interesting to observe how Anglo-Saxon writers, under the influence of Latin, the language of the books they read most, regarded it as entirely natural to admit Latin words into their own language. The principle of absorption was accepted from the beginning and the new words were made to conform to the existing patterns of the language. In *Beowulf*, for example, the only epic poem from the Anglo-Saxon period, the word *draca* 'dragon' coexists with the native word *wyrm*, probably introduced into the poet's vocabulary because of the needs of the alliterative metre. For this poet a sword was a *giganta geweorc* 'the work of giants' (L. *gīgas*, *gigantem*) and the men drank wine (*druncon win weras*) (L. *vīnum*) as well as beer and mead (both native words). (Robert Burchfield, *The English Language*, Oxford University Press 1985, p. 12)

A different sort of language specialist notes an early example of the principle of absorption in English which was to transform the language following the arrival of Norman French in 1066. Robert Burchfield, the editor of the revised *OED*, is the greatest lexicographer of our time, and his mastery of the English language is evident in the fastidious precision of his prose, in which there is no indication that he came originally from New Zealand. His admirable *New Fowler* is worth reading through not only for its sensible and unpedantic advice about usage, but for the impeccable SWE of Burchfield's comments and explanations.

8   LITERARY CRITICISM

Literary criticism, the critical analysis and evaluation of works of literature, now has two main streams: a traditional one, of ancient origin, which tends towards simple analysis, description, and appreciation; and another one, of relatively recent origin and now often described as 'theory', which is more technically analytical and is linked to branches of philosophy, sociology, and linguistics. Both streams are running strongly, the traditional one resulting in such things as critical biographies of writers, while the 'theory' is largely confined to academia.

As with language studies, the more traditional forms of literary criticism are written in SWE, while the modern technical developments use special concepts and vocabularies that can be difficult for non-specialists to understand and appreciate. These recent developments include, amongst others, New Criticism, Structuralism, Deconstruction, Feminist Criticism, and New Historicism.

Two traditional approaches to Mrs Gaskell's Wives and Daughters

Would not we sacrifice twenty Mollys for a single Cynthia?
Mrs Gaskell never asks herself such questions. The Victorian standards in which she had been educated told her that Molly was indisputably better than Cynthia. And she was no more capable of questioning these standards than she was of flying. The very idea, indeed, that she had stirred such questionings in her readers would have filled her with horrified dismay. But what are standards, however Victorian, against the lawless force of the sympathetic creative imagination? Mrs Gaskell made Cynthia a living human being because she could not help it. And it is the dangerous power of human beings like Cynthia to win our hearts and set our moral principles by the ears. (David Cecil, *Early Victorian Novelists*, London 1934; Pelican 1948, p. 168)

David Cecil's view of the Victorians was not unlike that of Lytton Strachey; and he saw Mrs Gaskell as a minor artist, limited by her femininity and her outlook, who created major fictional characters in spite of these disabilities. While his style is admirably clear, his tone is condescending, and he writes with an elegant, even precious, rhetoric that now seems as dated as his approach to the period. Ending the previous paragraph with a rhetorical question, including the arch inversion *would not we*, Cecil goes on to patronise: *she was no more capable of questioning these standards than she was of flying*. Then comes another rhetorical question, and the almost insulting *Mrs Gaskell made Cynthia a living human being because she could not help it*; and he ends by saying that girls like Cynthia – a fictional character – are a danger to our hearts and morals.

> Through Cynthia, Gaskell can leave Molly innocent yet show a girl fully aware of her developing sexual power: the reader can enjoy both the 'good' and the 'bad', Molly with her 'delicate neatness' and Cynthia with her 'tumbled gowns'. Their doubleness is suggested by Molly's immediate response to her stepsister; she 'fell in love with her, so to speak, on the instant' and 'would watch her perpetually as she went about the room, with the free stately grace of some wild animal in the forest'. It is natural that Roger Hamley should fall in love with both of them. At one stage Gaskell called her own Marianne both 'Molly' and 'Cynthia'. They are halves of a whole. (Jenny Uglow, *Elizabeth Gaskell: A Habit of Stories*, Faber, London 1993, p. 597)

Jenny Uglow shows a well-informed understanding both of Mrs Gaskell's artistry and of her ability to create character that is far deeper than David Cecil's, and she backs it up here with quotations from the novel, finding Molly just as interesting as Cynthia; they are indeed two halves of a whole, comparable in reality to her own daughters. Jenny Uglow's style is clear and accurate; but she refers to Mrs Gaskell either as 'Elizabeth' or as 'Gaskell'. This sounds false: Mrs Gaskell was called 'Lily', not Elizabeth, by most of those on Christian-name terms with her; and no one at all would have called her 'Gaskell', address by surname alone being used only between men; she would have done better to stick to 'Mrs Gaskell', or 'Elizabeth Gaskell'. (But in her later – and even more remarkable – biography of Hogarth she is right to refer to her subject as 'William' or 'Hogarth'.)

Modern critical theory (1): Explaining 'Deconstruction'

Derrida's central concept (although in principle it ought not to occupy such a 'hierarchical' position) is presented in his coining of the term *différance*, a French portmanteau word combining 'difference' with 'deferral' to suggest that the differential nature of meanings in language ceaselessly defers or postpones any determinate meaning: language is an endless chain or 'play of *différance*' which logocentric discourses try vainly to fix to some original or final term that can never be reached. Deconstructive readings track down within a text the aporia or internal contradiction that undermines its claims to coherent meaning: or they reveal how texts can be seen to deconstruct themselves. (Chris Baldick, *The Concise Oxford Dictionary of Literary Terms*, Oxford University Press 1990, p. 52)

This is as successful an attempt as can be expected to explain Deconstruction in a short space. Considering the number of technical and semi-technical terms he has to use (*hierarchical position*; *différance*; *portmanteau word*; *differential nature of meanings*; *determinate meaning*; *logocentric discourses*; *deconstructive readings*; *aporia*), Baldick's explanation of this nebulous and elusive theory is acceptably comprehensible; and he gives cross-references to further entries for '*différance*', 'portmanteau', and 'aporia'.

Now another scholar attempts the same task:

Derrida gives primacy to writing, where the realisation of the meaning is always postponed by the very fact that it will always be read and re-interpreted in the future. This fact separates the signified from the signifier temporally. The meaning is 'deferred', and Derrida coined the word 'différance' to express the dual spatial 'difference' and temporal 'deferment' detaching the sign from the full presence of its meaning. He denies that writing is secondary to speech or doubles the gap between *signifier* and *signified*. Where Rousseau regarded writing as a supplement to speech, Derrida sees it as both taking the place of speech and adding to it. (Harry Blamires, *A History of Literary Criticism*, Macmillan, London 1991, p. 363)

Blamires, writing a history rather than a dictionary, is easier to read than Baldick, but necessarily gets less into the same space; he makes a different approach, using a simpler SWE to explain Derrida's meaning. The result seems more transparent than the previous example, though it is not really much easier to understand; a problem that lies essentially with Derrida rather than with his interpreters. There are still a good many technical terms (*realisation of meaning*; *dual spatial 'difference' and temporal 'deferment'*; *the sign*), together with 'signifier' and 'signified' which have been explained already in the same chapter.

Modern critical theory (2): Rembrandt's 'The Anatomy Lesson'

The historical transformation which lies behind the palimpsestic impaction is not, however, evenly active in the image, and it is the modernising pole of its dialectic which is dominant and therefore 'spontaneously' visible today. ... If the painting's aesthetic is a realism, its social valency is given in those grave bourgeois faces, avid or complacent, which stare across and out of the frame. They too are strangely paradoxical: on the threshold of an epistemological journey into the modern, and yet frozen eternally in a solidarity of prestige, learning and prosperity (although the fact that each had paid to be present in the depiction may only serve to make us unduly cynical about the inner principle of such a collectivity). They represent at once new historical movement, and its hypostatization, for, stylistically in touch with the plethora of other group portraits in which this bourgeoisie, in its first ascendancy, celebrated and had represented its own solidity – as epistemological as it is political and social – the painting seeks to portray not merely some random scene, some historical anecdote (although any realism must always run this risk) but an episode charged with the semiosis of the new power, represented, however, as an already achieved, and indeed eternal fact. (Francis Barker, *The Tremulous Private Body*, Methuen, London 1984, pp. 76–7)

Although this extract concerns a picture, it comes from a book by a literary critic in which various art forms are considered. It is not easy to read; but somewhere behind the abstruse language of 'theory' lurks a competent writer. Barker's handling of the basic language – his accurate sentence-structure, and his choice and usage of ordinary words – demonstrate his skill; even the structure of the over-long last sentence beginning *They represent at once* ... is just acceptable; but the whole is made impenetrable by the jargon. At an average of two jargon terms per sentence, such words as *palimpsestic*; *impaction*; *modernising pole*; *dialectic*; *valency*; *epistemological*; *collectivity*; *hypostatization*;

semiosis effectively thwart, not comprehension – for the words can be looked up in a dictionary[9] – but the desire to comprehend.

9 PHILOSOPHY

Philosophy, the search for truth and the nature of reality, includes the theory of knowledge, metaphysics (theories of mind, meaning, and causality), and ethics (theories of morals in human conduct). It has occupied thinkers from the earliest times, and the subject continues to develop in its various branches, and to engage its practitioners. The examples given here concern ethics.

Kant and Russell on the 'categorical imperative', or ultimate moral law

Russell quotes Kant

'If I think of a categorical imperative, I know at once what it contains. For as the imperative contains, besides the Law, only the necessity of the maxim to be in accordance with this law, but the Law contains no condition by which it is limited, nothing remains over but the generality of a law in general, to which the maxim of the action is to be conformable, and which conforming alone presents the imperative as necessary. Therefore the categorical imperative is a single one, and in fact this: *Act only according to a maxim by which you can at the same time will that it shall become a general law.*' Or: '*Act as if the maxim of your action were to become through your will a general natural law.*'

Russell goes on to comment on this quotation

Kant gives as an illustration of the working of the categorical imperative that it is wrong to borrow money, because if we all tried to do so there would be no money left to borrow. One can in like manner show that theft and murder are condemned by the categorical imperative. But there are some acts which Kant would certainly think wrong but which cannot be shown to be wrong by his principles, for instance suicide; it would be quite possible for a melancholic to wish that everybody should commit suicide. His

9. Only *semiosis* is omitted from both *Collins* and *COD*; but it can be found in *OED*.

maxim seems, in fact, to give a necessary but not a sufficient criterion of virtue. To get a *sufficient* criterion, we should have to abandon Kant's purely formal point of view, and take some account of the effects of actions. Kant, however, states emphatically that virtue does not depend upon the intended result of a action, but only on the principle of which it is itself a result; and if this is conceded, nothing more concrete than his maxim is possible. (Bertrand Russell, *History of Western Philosophy*, Allen and Unwin, London 1946, pp. 737–8)

The quotation from Kant is a grim example of philosophical exposition that is dense to the point of near-incomprehensibility, even though it concerns a matter that should be comprehensible, and is relatively free of jargon; the over-long second sentence has to be read very carefully, and probably more than once, if it is to be construed. Russell's style of explaining philosophy is the very opposite of this, as he comments on what Kant has said in simple, lucid prose.[10]

Mary Warnock summarises F. H. Bradley's answer to the question 'Why should I be moral?'

His solution is that the good is self-realization, and that this is the end or purpose of the moral man's life. At first he seeks to establish this by an appeal to moral consciousness. He takes for granted that there is a certain set of facts with which everyone is acquainted, such as the fact that we often feel ourselves to be under some obligation, or that we often feel that morally we have failed in some way. To these facts, or rather our knowledge of them, he refers as moral consciousness. He raises no question about the scope of morality, or the application of moral concepts. These things are accepted as the data on which the moral philosopher has to work. This unquestioning attitude to the supposed facts of our moral life, and the appeal to such arbiters as 'pleasure', 'duty', 'moral consciousness', all absolutely in general, makes Bradley's writing seem at times fantastically abstract and difficult to connect with any single particular

10. For more on Russell's prose, see pp. 42–7 above.

phenomenon. But in this generality also lies its power, since if his account seems explanatory at all, it seems explanatory of every aspect of life. (Mary Warnock, *Ethics Since 1900*, 2nd edn, Oxford University Press, 1966, p. 2)

Mary Warnock's summary of Bradley's ethical thinking is clarity itself, lacking any elaboration, and much less woolly than some of Bradley's ideas; but she confesses that she finds some of his terms incomprehensible: 'It is not clear what is meant by "realizing" the self, let alone realizing it "as a whole"'. She goes on: 'though it is easy either to be put off by the unclarities, or to stop trying to understand, and simply to drift along with the style as one reads, it is all the same possible to detect in Bradley's theory something which is important and is very often at the back of people's minds when they talk about morality' (p. 3).[11]

A contemporary philosopher considers morality

As Kant himself pointed out, the moral law has an absolute character. Rights cannot be arbitrarily overridden, or weighed against the profit of ignoring them. Duties cannot be arbitrarily set aside or cancelled by the bad results of due obedience. I must respect your right, regardless of conflicting interests, since you alone can renounce or cancel it. That is the point of the concept – to provide an absolute barrier against invasion. A right is an interest that is given special protection, and which cannot be overridden or cancelled without the consent of the person who possesses it. By describing an interest as a right we lift it from the account of cost and benefit, and place it in the sacred precinct of the self. (Roger Scruton, *An Intelligent Person's Guide to Philosophy*, Duckworth, London 1996, p. 112)

This paragraph is easy and pleasant to read because it is written with great care and precision, and with a feeling for the beauty that is inherent in simple English; English enhanced by the underlying metaphorical content of words such as 'overridden',

11. Is Bradley thinking, perhaps, of the 'self-realisation', or transcendental understanding, that is aimed at by the mystics of all the great religions, and is referred to by that name by such great Hindu mystics as Ramakrishna and Ramana Maharshi?

'weighed', 'barrier', 'invasion', and by the overt (if slightly mixed) metaphor of the last sentence. Notice too how the 'personality' or 'flavour' of Scruton's philosophical prose differs from those of Russell and Mary Warnock in the preceding extracts.

What is most notable about the philosophical prose of Russell, Mary Warnock, and Scruton is its wonderful clarity and simplicity. One reason for this is that they were all writing more for laymen than for other philosophers; but the reason why it was possible for them to write in this way was that, in order to practise their sort of philosophy effectively, they had to be able to think clearly and to express their thoughts simply.

10 SOCIOLOGY AND PSYCHOLOGY

Sociology and psychology are two of the disciplines that make most use of jargon. It is easy to make fun of gobbledygook – one has only to think of the article written in dense but meaningless jargon that was recently submitted as a spoof and seriously accepted for publication by a professional journal in America – but it need not delay us here. Instead we shall look at examples of sociological and psychological writing that make real attempts to be comprehensible.

Order in modern society

Tönnies and Durkheim wrote of a 'loss of community' in industrial societies at a time when the socially disruptive effects of industrialization were highly conspicuous and before welfare state policies had been widely introduced to improve matters. Their observations are perceptive and relevant as a comparison between their own and pre-industrial times, but they clearly cannot be regarded as a final statement on the nature of modern society. A telling criticism of the 'loss of community' thesis is that it pessimistically under-estimates the ability of human beings to express their needs and feelings in new ways by developing or adapting institutions. Thus, for the young in modern society, the peer group is often more important for expressive purposes than neighbourhood, friends and kin, excluding immediate kin. In any case, working-class communities did strongly re-emerge in most industrial towns. Further, it is arguable that the modern nuclear family provides emotional support just as readily as the extended family, albeit for fewer people, and that the modern home is well equipped to enable family members to express many of their interests and feelings. (Mike O'Donnell, 'Social order, social change and socialization', in *Fundamentals of Sociology*, ed. Patrick McNeill and Charles Townley, 2nd edn, Thornes of Cheltenham, 1986, p. 115)

This extract is not at all difficult to understand. The technical terms are few and of a sort that is recognised by most people (*peer group*; *nuclear family*; *extended family*), and the grammar is unexceptionable. Yet the prose style – more than the content – is somehow dull and fails to make its subject seem interesting; pages of the stuff, one feels, would be soporific. Why is this? The extract is in the first place verbose, saying what it has to say in more words than necessary; for instance *the ability of human beings to express their needs and feelings in new ways by developing or adapting institutions* (nineteen words) does not really say much more than 'people's ability to adapt themselves by changing their circumstances' (nine words). Secondly it employs slack stock phrases (*highly conspicuous*; *final statement*; *telling criticism*; *the young*; *expressive purposes*). And thirdly there is a leaden plod to the exposition; take the second sentence: *Their observations are perceptive and relevant as a comparison between their own and pre-industrial times, but they clearly cannot be regarded as a final statement on the nature of modern society*, where *as a comparison between* would have been better expressed as 'for comparing', and where the observations of Tönnies and Durkheim, writing at the end of the nineteenth century, cannot be expected to make a final, or any other, statement about modern society.

Trouble on the terraces

A complex society usually includes a number of micro-societies whose ways of assigning meaning to their actions are not universally nor even very widely shared in the community. In such a situation the possibility exists for attributions of meaning to be made to the deeds of members of the microsociety which bear little resemblance to the meanings attributed by the members themselves. An intuition that this is indeed so may be very difficult to substantiate if the attributions made by members of the dominant society are very loud and very visible, and those of the members of the microsociety hard to come by, perhaps because those members are not easy to contact. There are many examples of this situation in contemporary Britain, such as the case of some schoolchildren, many gypsies and almost all football fans. (Peter Marsh, Elisabeth Rosser, and Rom Harré, *The Rules of Disorder*, Routledge and Kegan Paul, London 1978, repr. 1987, p. 4)

This is written in a much better quality of prose than that of the last extract. Apart from the special uses of the words *attribution* and *meaning*, it is both comprehensible, and tightly and interestingly written. If we were to substitute 'understanding of' for *ways of assigning meaning to* in the first sentence, and 'judgements to be made of' for *attributions of meaning to be made to* in the second, and so on, it would be an acceptable piece of SWE.

According to Freud

If a person had developed a certain amount of castration anxiety or anxiety over loss of love, and subsequently has overcome this anxiety by certain inner reassurances ('It is not so bad after all, and probably there is no real castration, and I shall not be abandoned for good'), the experience of a trauma is apt to upset these reassurances and to re-mobilise the old anxieties. Persons who, for example, have hitherto denied their fears by partial regression to the security of primitive narcissism and omnipotence are forced by the trauma to admit that they are not omnipotent after all, and the old anxieties reappear. This is especially true in one type of anxiety over loss of love. Some persons have the capacity for hanging on to the belief that fate will protect them, just as their parents had protected them before in their childhood. Such persons experience a trauma as a betrayal by fate which refuses to protect them any longer. The frightening idea of having lost the protection of a powerful person with superego qualities varies in intensity according to the degree to which the subject had already submitted to a passive-receptive attitude before experiencing the trauma. (Otto Fenichel, *The Psychoanalytic Theory of Neurosis*, Routledge and Kegan Paul, London 1946, repr. 1990, p. 123)

Again we have a passage that is easy to read and comprehend provided that a few key technical terms are understood (*castration anxiety*; *trauma*; *narcissism and omnipotence*; *superego*; *passive-receptive*). What is interesting here is that the jargon of Freudian psychoanalysis has been so thoroughly absorbed into the language that most people will understand all these terms, more or less, though *superego qualities* (meaning here 'qualities that can impose social rules') might give some a moment's pause. Otherwise, whatever one thinks of the theory, the writing is notably clear.

11   RELIGION

Religious texts are among the very oldest writings; and the development of the English language has been profoundly affected from the sixteenth century onwards by the language of the Bible and the liturgy. Until recent times the language of the 1611 ('King James') Bible and the 1662 Prayer Book, which had sixteenth-century roots, was that normally used both in and out of church; but, starting with the Revised Version of the Bible (1881–5), and the 1928 Prayer Book, the old forms have been gradually abandoned and replaced by modernised versions in correct, if sometimes uninspiring, SWE. However, the word of God is attended to nowadays by fewer worshippers than it used to be, and these changes are unlikely to have much effect on the language.

There is a great deal of other religious writing, including apologetics, Christology, church history, commentaries, exegesis, hagiography, mysticism, prayers, sermons, theology, and so on. Here we have examples written by an intellectual interested in spiritual beliefs, a Christian layman, and a scientist.

The spiritual value of silence

Unrestrained and indiscriminate talk is morally evil and spiritually dangerous. 'But I say unto you, That every idle word that men shall speak, they shall give account thereof in the day of judgment.' This may seem a very hard saying.

And yet if we pass in review the words we have given vent to in the course of a an average day, we shall find that the greater number of them may be classified under three main heads: words inspired by malice and uncharitableness towards our neighbours; words inspired by greed, sensuality and self-love; words inspired by pure imbecility and uttered without rhyme or reason, but merely for the sake of making a distracting noise. These are idle words; and we shall find, if we look into the matter, that they tend to outnumber the words that are dictated by reason, charity or necessity. And if the unspoken words of our mind's endless, idiot monologue are counted, the majority for idleness becomes, for most of us, overwhelmingly large. (Aldous Huxley, *The Perennial Philosophy*, Chatto and Windus, London 1946, pp. 247–8)

In his recapitulation of insights from the great mysticisms of the world, Huxley sometimes adopts, as he does in the first sentence here, the voice of a prophet, backing it up with a quotation from Matthew; and indeed we do talk a lot of rubbish, much of it ill-natured. Huxley was always inclined to oracular pronouncements, even in his novels, but his use of language, with its flavour of the interwar intellectual, was precise and flexible. Here he reviews our shortcomings in balanced, schoolmasterly prose, slightly marred only by the hyperbolical *pure imbecility* and the cliché *without rhyme or reason*.

The problem of pain

'If God were good, He would wish to make his creatures perfectly happy, and if God were almighty He would be able to do what He wished. But the creatures are not happy. Therefore God lacks either goodness, or power, or both.' This is the problem of pain, in its simplest form. The possibility of answering it depends on showing that the terms 'good' and 'almighty', and perhaps also the term 'happy' are equivocal: for it must be admitted from the outset that if the popular meanings attached to these words are the best, or the only possible, meanings, then the argument is unanswerable. (C. S. Lewis, *The Problem of Pain*, Geoffrey Bles, London 1940, p. 14)

With simplicity and clarity, Lewis presents a problem which must puzzle anyone who considers moral philosophy in a theological context. Another way of putting the question is 'Why do the innocent have to suffer in calamities both natural and man-made?' Why Aberfan? Why genocide? With an honesty that gives his argument its strength, Lewis admits straight away that it is unanswerable in his formulation unless 'good', 'almighty', and perhaps 'happy' are given new meanings, rather than the usual ones; so that in the other formulation of the question 'innocent', 'suffer', and perhaps 'calamity' also have to be redefined if a theologically satisfactory answer is to be found. As Humpty Dumpty said, 'A word means just what I choose it to mean'.

Science, the 'how', and the 'why'

Most scientists have a deep distrust of mysticism. This is not surprising, as mystical thought lies at the opposite extreme to rational thought, which is the basis of the scientific method. Also, mysticism tends to be confused with the occult, the paranormal, and other fringe beliefs. In fact, many of the world's finest thinkers, including some notable scientists such as Einstein, Pauli, Schrödinger, Heisenberg, Eddington, and Jeans, have also espoused mysticism. My own feeling is that the scientific method should be pursued as far as it possibly can. Mysticism is no substitute for scientific inquiry and logical reasoning so long as this approach can be consistently applied. It is only in dealing with ultimate questions that science and logic may fail us. I am not saying that science and logic are likely to provide the wrong answers, but they may be incapable of addressing the sort of 'why' (as opposed to 'how') questions we want to ask. (Paul Davies, *The Mind of God: Science and the Search for Ultimate Meaning*, London 1992, Penguin, p. 226)

Paul Davies, a professor of mathematical physics at an Australian university (although he is English by origin), finishes his book with a fair account from the scientist's point of view of the relationship of science to mysticism. He writes a very simple, easily understood prose (though there is an awkward construction in the second half of the last sentence), which distinguishes the best books written by scientists for non-scientists. It is characteristic of such works that the 'paranormal' is dismissed as a 'fringe belief', despite the actual paranormal experiences of many, perhaps most, people (presumably including scientists who manage not to believe in them).

12   TECHNOLOGY AND COMPUTING

Technological writing inevitably involves much special terminology and often includes mathematics. Nevertheless there are normally parts of a technological text that can be expressed in relatively unspecialised terms – for which SWE is available – and it is with these that we are concerned here. We begin with a history of windmill technology:

Modern windfarms

In Britain, some use is being made of windpower to generate electricity. In 1982 on Fair Isle, a three-bladed 50 kW generator was installed with a rotor diameter of 14 m (46 ft.). Not only has this reduced electricity bills, as it has partially supplanted a diesel generator, but the islanders no longer fear the prospect of winter storms cutting them off from essential oil supplies. Similarly in Shetland, in 1988 a 750 kW wind turbine was phased in. It was built by James Howden & Co. Ltd. and, with a rotor diameter of 45 m (147 ft. 8 in.); it is the largest three-bladed turbine in the United Kingdom. The control system, which is operated remotely from the diesel generating station at Lerwick 30 km (18.6 miles) away, works through spoilers at the tips of the blades and is based on two programmable logic controllers which regulate the operating and monitoring functions of the machine including the run up and shut down. It will generate with wind speeds between 4.91 and 25 m/sec. (11 to 56 m.p.h.), or up to a force ten storm. The load builds up until a wind speed of 12.96 m/sec. (29 m.p.h.) is reached, at which speed the full 750 kW is produced. (Richard L. Hills, *Power from Wind: A History of Windmill Technology*, Cambridge University Press 1994, pp. 277–8)

No one is going to find this passage – which is aimed at windmill enthusiasts as well as engineers – hard to understand (guessing that a *programmable logic controller* is some sort of computerised control system); and anyone who wonders how the local windfarm works is going to find it interesting. The prose is simple, clear, accurate, and slightly plodding – though the copy-editor has missed the semicolon in the sentence beginning *It was built by James Howden ...*, which ought to be a comma – and the technological effect is chiefly the result of the clusters of metric measurements, with their non-metric equivalents dutifully added in parentheses.

Image analysis in television

Because a picture has two dimensions it is only possible to transmit all the information contained within it in *serial* form, if we are to use but one wire or RF channel to carry the signal. This implies a *dissection* process, and requires a timing element to define the rate of analysis; this timing element must be present at both sending and receiving ends so that the analysis of the image at the sending end, and the simultaneous build-up of the picture at the receiver, occur in synchronism. Thus a television picture may be dissected in any manner, provided that the receiver assembles its picture in precisely the same way; but the path link between sender and viewer must contain *two* distinct information streams: video signal, which is an electrical analogy of the light pattern being sent, and timing signals, or synchronis-ation pulses, to define the steps in the dissection process. The presence of a timing element suggests that each picture will take a certain period to be built up; how long will depend on how quickly we can serialise the picture *elements*, and this in turn depends on the bandwidth available in the transmission system – more of this later. (Eugene Trundle, *Guide to TV and Video Technology*, 2nd edn, Newnes, Oxford 1996, p. 1)

This is the beginning of a technical manual which soon plunges into the circuit diagrams, statistics, and jargon of electrical en-gineering; but, throughout, the author keeps as far as possible to the plain but comprehensible prose of his opening, and there is no reason why it should not be understood by anyone who is capable of GCSE science. It is frankly an instruction book, the key words, to which a teacher would give emphasis and of which a student would be expected to take notes, being italicised; and it is equipped with clear diagrams and illustrations.

Electronic languages

The computer treats language as it treats logic, space, and time – with an odd combination of practicality and philosophical abstraction. On the practical level, computer languages are codes whose purpose is to represent the logical structure of problems to be solved. They are removed as far as possible from the emotional, ambiguous, and vocalised language of everyday life. And yet they are not without traditions ... In creating his codes, the computer specialist in fact takes part in a debate that has been lively for thousands of years. Should language evoke or simply denote? Does it enter into a magical or at least mysterious relationship with the thoughts and experiences it describes, or is it primarily a tool for laying bare the structure of the world? Is language essentially poetic or logical? As we look first at computer language itself, then at the traditions of which it is a part, we shall not be surprised to see which side the computer favors in this debate. Poets, philosophers, and computer programmers may agree that language provides a path to knowledge. They do not agree on the nature of language or the kind of knowledge to which it leads. (J. David Bolter, *Turing's Man*, North Carolina University Press 1984, ch. 8)

This beginning of a chapter on computer languages is written by an American professor of Canadian origin – could you tell that he was American before you came to *favors*? – in an accomplished, elegant SWE. There is a pleasing rhetorical flourish in the three successive questions put to set the terms of the debate about the nature of language, and no metaphors other than *a path to knowledge*. This is good academic SWE, far removed from the illiterate convolutions that can occur in computer literature.

13   SCIENCE

Even more than with technology, the professional writings of scientists, which are chiefly published in journals such as *Nature*, are couched in highly technical, often symbolic, language, and frequently cannot be understood by lay readers – or even by scientists working in other fields. But there is another sort of writing by scientists which is just as reputable but which is aimed at non-scientists, and it is this sort of popular science from which the following examples are taken.[12]

Otto Frisch, born an Austrian, writes in English about atomic particles

Let me first recapitulate what is known about the structure of atoms. Since 1911 we have known that each atom consists of a heavy core or nucleus, surrounded by a number of much lighter particles called electrons. Different atoms have different kinds of nuclei, but electrons are all alike. Electrons all weigh the same and have the same negative electric charge, but an atom is not electrically charged, the negative charge of its electron being offset by an equal positive charge of the nucleus. To put it another way round: the nucleus has a positive charge which is Z times the charge of an electron; hence Z electrons become arranged around the nucleus to form an atom, which is electrically neutral (i.e. uncharged). (Otto Frisch, 'Atomic Particles', *Science Survey I*, London 1960; quoted in John Carey, *The Faber Book of Science*, Faber, London 1995, pp. 403–4)

The English here is so fresh and plain that it is impossible to guess that its author's first language was German (though Frisch had worked for the previous twenty years in England and America). The science itself is not very difficult to understand, but it is explained with scrupulous simplicity, each technical term being defined as it occurs.

Chaotic motion and strange attractors

Suppose a particle is moving in a confined region of space according to a definite deterministic law. Following the path traced out by the particle, we are likely to observe that

12. A master of popular science was J. B. S. Haldane, whose essay 'On Being the Right Size' is a classic of the genre (in *On Being the Right Size and Other Essays*, ed. John Maynard Smith, Oxford 1985).

it settles down to one of three possible behaviours – the geometrical description of which is called an attractor. The particle may be attracted to a final resting position (like, for example, the bob on a pendulum as it gradually settles down to rest). In this case, the attractor is just a point – the final resting position of the bob. Or the particle may settle down in a periodic cycle (like the planets in their orbits around the Sun). Here the attractor is an ellipse and the future motion can be predicted with astonishingly high accuracy as far ahead as we want. The last possibility is that the particle may continue to move wildly and erratically while, nevertheless, remaining in some bounded region of space. The motion of some of the asteroids, for example, appears to exhibit exactly this phenomenon. Tiny inaccuracies in measuring the position and speed of the asteroid quickly lead to enormous errors in predicting its future path. This phenomenon is the signal of chaotic motion. The regions of space traced out by such motions are called strange attractors. (Caroline Series, *The New Scientist Guide to Chaos*, ed. Nina Hall, London 1991, quoted in John Carey, *The Faber Book of Science*, Faber, London 1995, p. 496)

This paragraph forms part of an explanation of the mathematical meaning of chaos. Despite some specialised vocabulary – the term *strange attractors* is really too elegant to be called jargon – this is an account that is readily understandable because of the simple, clear construction of the prose and of the apposite examples that the author gives to illustrate the various motions she describes. This and the previous example are comparable in style and clarity with the extracts in section 9 on philosophy, above.

The wonder of eye and brain

The eye sends, as we saw, in to the cell-and-fibre forest of the brain throughout the waking day continual rhythmic streams of tiny, individually evanescent, electrical potentials. This throbbing, streaming crowd of electrified shifting points in the spongework of the brain bears no obvious semblance in space-pattern, and even in temporal relation resembles but a little remotely the tiny two-dimensional upside-down picture of the outside world which the eyeball paints on the beginnings of its nerve fibres to the brain. But that little picture sets up an electrical storm. And that electrical storm so set up is one which affects a whole population of brain-cells. Electrical charges having in themselves not the faintest elements of the visual – having, for instance, nothing of 'distance', 'right-side-upness', nor 'vertical, nor 'horizontal', nor 'colour', nor 'brightness', nor 'shadow', nor 'roundness', nor 'squareness', nor 'contour', nor 'transparency', nor 'opacity, nor 'near', nor 'far', nor visual anything – conjure up all these. (Sir Charles Sherrington, *Man on His Nature*, 2nd edn, Cambridge 1951, quoted in John Carey, *The Faber Book of Science*, Faber, London 1995, pp. 316–17)

Perhaps the wonder evident in every line of Sherrington's account is less exciting now that electrical charges stored in computers can produce 'virtual reality', but it is still wonderful that visual images can be extracted from electrical impulses however it is done. In any case, Sherrington's ardent rhetoric – including the catalogue of visual effects produced in the human brain from the tiny electrical impulses from the eye – still excites a matching wonder in the reader. Again there are scarcely any technical terms, and nothing that non-scientists would find difficult.

14 SWE AND NATIONALITY

To see whether it is possible to tell the nationalities of accomplished practitioners of SWE from the way they write, here are the beginnings of five essays by five authors of different nationalities about episodes in James Joyce's *Ulysses*.[13] The authors, all of them Joyce scholars, are – but not in this order – an American, an Australian, an Englishman, a German-Swiss, and a Scot; and their essays were all copy-edited at the same time to the same standard. The question is, does anything in their writing reveal their nationalities?

13. *James Joyce's Ulysses: Critical Essays*, ed. Clive Hart and David Hayman, University of California Press, Berkeley and London 1974.

a. [Aeolus] A crucial event takes place at this point in the narrative: Bloom does some work. Work in *Ulysses* is a rare process. There is plenty of activity, many miles are travelled, many elbows raised, but bread-winning productive work, 'servile' work of the kind that may not be performed on the Sabbath, is minimal. Barmaids, curates, whores, and beggars ply their trades, and in the background there are glimpses of the navvies, draymen, and tramwaymen who represent the labouring classes of Dublin. Stephen does a nominal hour as schoolmaster, taking a class from 10 to 11 (if that can be called work), and is duly paid. (p. 115)

b. [Wandering Rocks] After the mind-stuff of 'Scylla and Charybdis', with its indoor setting, we pass to the open-air physical world of the city. While the contrast is obvious, there is also a sense of continuity. As Mr Kellogg points out, Joyce felt it important to hold to the now, the here, as the essential 'classical' basis from which all flights of artistic imagination might begin. 'Wandering Rocks', following immediately on Stephen's theorising, is Joyce's most direct, most complete celebration of Dublin, demonstrating succinctly his conception of the importance of physical reality, meticulously documented, as the soil from which fictions may best grow. (p. 181)

c. [Nausicaa] The last scene of the preceding chapter transfigured Leopold Bloom and projected him skyward at a specified and ballistically advantageous angle. The ascendant curve is continued into the first part of 'Nausicaa', which gratifyingly exalts Bloom, at least as viewed from the favourable angle of one observer, from a particularly one-eyed, romanticized perspective. The observer, Gerty MacDowell, herself intently watched by Bloom, is in turn portrayed at her spectacular best, with fulsome touches and lavish colours. In addition, both she and Bloom are emotionally and physiologically exalted. 'Nausicaa' is a chapter of culminations, of aspirations and high expectations, of sky-gazing and firework-gazing, of ecstatic flights and raised limbs. (p. 277)

d. [Oxen of the Sun] This chapter is an exercise in imitative form. Joyce is trying to make words reproduce objects and processes. The reader is confronted in the three opening paragraphs with an example of this technique employed for the traditional purpose of setting the place. The three paragraphs, each with threefold repetition, form a verbal equivalent for Homer's island of Trinacria, literally 'Three headlands' or, as it is described in Lamb's *Adventures of Ulysses*, 'having three promontories jutting into the sea'.

Perhaps Joyce deliberately made the opening difficult to understand in order to warn his readers that what follows requires careful reading. (p. 313)

e. [Ithaca] If *Ulysses* is a crucial testing ground for theories of the novel, as it seems to have become, the 'Ithaca' episode must be a *locus classicus* for every critic interested in the traditions of English and European fiction. Here the extremes of Joyce's art, and of fiction in general, are found in radical form: the tension between symbolism and realism, what Arnold Goldman has called the 'myth/fact paradox', gives the episode its essential life. Joyce once told Frank Budgen that 'Ithaca' was his 'favourite episode', the 'ugly duckling of the book', and his frequent references to the episode in his letters reveal a personal and artistic involvement seldom matched in his work on the other chapters. (p. 385)

The nationalities of the five authors are in fact: *a* Scottish (Matthew Hodgart); *b* Australian (Clive Hart); *c* German-Swiss (Fritz Senn); *d* English (J. S. Atherton); and *e* American (A. Walton Litz); but I can find no clear indication of their nationalities in the ways that they write. Their personal styles, however, are quite distinct from each other, as can be seen by comparing Matthew Hodgart's ironical, laid-back prose (*a*) with Clive Hart's down-to-earth simplicity (*b*), with Fritz Senn's extravagance (*c*), with J. S. Atherton's precision (*d*), and with the elegance of A. Walton Litz (*e*).

Afterword

Let us look again, finally, at the four propositions that were made at the beginning of the book. They were:

1. that SWE exists, and that it is worth an English-speaker's while to learn how to use it;
2. that even the most abstruse concepts can be expounded in language so simple, clear, and free of unnecessary jargon that anyone who is capable of comprehending the subject can follow it without difficulty;
3. that the written language, just as much as the spoken language, is not static but changes and develops; and
4. that each person's prose style can be as individual and attractive – or unattractive – as any other facet of his or her personality.

Have these propositions been supported by the arguments in Parts I and II, and by the examples in Parts III and IV? I think that they have. First, most of the examples, though written by people of different periods and backgrounds whose spoken English would not have been the same, have numerous similarities of form which confirm the existence of SWE; and this conclusion is reinforced by the last set of examples ('SWE and Nationality'), where it is obvious that scholars from five different countries are all writing in the same dialect. This is indeed a common language that is plainly worth learning. Secondly, the clarity with which the philosophical concepts in Part III (Russell) and in Part IV.9 (Philosophy) are explained, and which is found in several other technical examples, shows that difficult subjects can be explained in simple language – though other writers can obfuscate what should be plain (for instance the quotations from Kant in Part IV.9 and from Barker in Part IV.8). Thirdly, there are examples in the section on vocabulary, Part I.2, and in Part IV.7 (Language) which illustrate changes occurring over time to the meanings of written words and phrases. Finally, it is clear in the extracts from the four stylists in Part III, as well as in the examples in Part IV, that the prose of a writer of SWE does usually have a distinct flavour or personality, which varies considerably from writer to writer.

Appendix
The Story of the English Language

by R. W. Burchfield

1   OLD ENGLISH: *c*.740 AD TO 1066

The English language began its life in the speech of Germanic tribesmen living in Frisia and neighbouring territories. In the fifth century AD some of these tribes, all speaking closely related but not identical dialects, came to the British Isles. They spread out over much of the country, driving the Celtic-speaking Britons back to the western and northern fringes. From Celtic speakers they adopted many place-names and place-name elements (e.g. *cumb* valley, *torr* rocky peak), but only a handful of general words (e.g. *bannoc* a piece (of cake or loaf), *brocc* badger, *dunn* dun).

Most of the Germanic newcomers were illiterate but their rune-masters brought with them an alphabet called the runic alphabet or *futhorc* (named from the first six characters, *feorh* wealth, *ur* aurochs, *thorn* thorn, *os* ?mouth, *rad* riding, and *cen* torch). The runes were scratched or carved on many objects as indications of ownership or of fabrication, or for some other practical or ornamental purpose.

These runic characters gave way to the Roman alphabet when Christian missionaries arrived at the end of the sixth century, and the language of the dominant Anglo-Saxon tribes was forced into this new alphabet. Only the thorn (the Old English version of *th*), wynn (= *w*), and ash (written *æ*, the vowel equivalent to that in modern English *cat*) survived from the runic alphabet.

The earliest English written in the Roman alphabet is found in

Reprinted by permission of Oxford University Press from *Oxford English: A Guide to the Language*, compiled by I. C. B. Dear, Oxford University Press 1986, pp. 3–17.

a manuscript of *c*.737 AD. One of the poems in the manuscript, a Northumbrian version of Caedmon's *Hymn*, shows common Old English words in their earliest form (e.g. *uard* later *weard* 'guardian', *eci dryctin* later *ece dryhten* 'eternal lord').

By coming to Britain, the newcomers, who at an early stage called themselves 'English', separated themselves in nationality and language from their European counterparts for ever, though it could not have been evident to them at the time. The first great severance of the western Germanic languages had occurred. At some point between the fifth and the eleventh centuries an independent language called English became clearly distinguishable – independent, that is, from the other Germanic tribal languages, those that later came to be called Dutch, German, Danish, Icelandic, and so on.

The vocabulary of Old English is almost entirely Germanic. Nouns, which fell clearly into numerous demonstrably different declensions, also possessed grammatical gender (masculine, feminine, or neuter) and were inflected according to case (nominative, accusative, genitive, and dative) and number. Nouns in the dative case were sometimes, but not always, preceded by a preposition. Verbs, then as now, fell into three main classes, called by modern grammarians strong (in which the past tense is formed by a change of internal vowel, for example, OE *rīdan*, *rād*, modE *ride*, *rode*); weak (in which the past tense is formed in modE by the addition of -*ed*, for example, OE *cyssan*, *cyssede*, modE *kiss*, *kissed*); and irregular (OE *bēon*, *gān*, etc., modE *be*, *go*, etc.). Adjectives and most of the numbers were inflected according to certain obligatory rules. The numbering system changed after the number 60 (*þrītig* 30, *fēowertig* 40, *fīftig* 50, *siextig* 60, but *hundseofontig* 70, *hundeahtatig* 80). The subjunctive mood and impersonal constructions were obligatory in many more circumstances than they are now. There was no future tense. Periphrastic verbal forms of the type 'he was coming' were exceedingly rare. Dialectal variation was extremely complicated. Nearly all of the written work that has survived is literary (especially alliterative poetry), documentary (charters, wills, etc.), or religious (homilies): in other words formal in content and elevated in style. The form of English used in the daily conversations of Anglo-Saxons has not survived.

After the arrival of St Augustine in Canterbury in AD 597, and the gradual adoption of Christianity in most parts of the country, the language began to absorb some Latin words. A few Latin words had even made their way into the tribal homelands of the Germanic peoples before our ancestors moved to Britain, among them *mint* (OE *mynet* coin), *pound* (OE *pund*), and *street* (OE *strǣt*). In the Christian period a much larger group of Latin words appeared in the language for the first time, among them *cook* (OE *cōc*), *font* (OE *font*), *pope* (OE *pāpa*), and *school* (OE *scōl*, from medL *scōla*, L. *schola*).

In the later part of the Anglo-Saxon period, Old English also acquired many expressions from Scandinavian sources when Danish soldiers, and later settlers, crossed the North Sea to this country. The poems and chronicles of the later Anglo-Saxon period show words of Scandinavian origin like *dreng* 'warrior', *niðing* 'villain', *cnearr* 'a small ship', and *scegð* 'a light ship'. The settling down of the Danes is reflected in other loan-words – *husbonda* 'householder, husband', *feolaga* 'fellow', *grið* 'peace', and, perhaps most important of all, *lagu* 'law'. Three of the commonest Old English verbs were gradually superseded by their Scandinavian equivalents: as time went on *call* (late OE *ceallian*, ON *kalla*) slowly displaced OE *hātan* and *clipian*; *take* (late OE *tacan*, ON *taka*) superseded OE *niman* in its main senses, leaving *nim* only in the restricted sense 'steal'; and *cast* (early ME *casten*, ON *kasta*) slowly displaced OE *weorpan* in the sense 'throw'.

2   MIDDLE ENGLISH: 1066 TO 1476

The dates are somewhat arbitrary: 1066 is the year of the Battle of Hastings and the arrival of the Normans, and 1476 is chosen as the year in which printing was introduced in England by William Caxton.

From 1066 for nearly three hundred years the official language of the British Isles was French, though English remained the ordinary spoken language of the majority of the population.

During this period the influence of Norman French was strong enough for it to bring an ordinal numeral (*second*) into English to replace the traditional Old English one (*other*, OE *ōþer*). The phonetic contribution was somewhat more substantial. For example, numerous words came into English with the diphthong -*oi*- (or -*oy*), a very rare combination in the system developed from native Old English words. Many such words, for example *choice*, *cloister*, *coy*, *employ*, *exploit*, *joy*, *loyal*, *noise*, *poise*, *royal*, and *voyage*, came into English then.

But the main development was the replacement of a large number of Old English words by more or less synonymous French words. The old patterns of behaviour and of social codification of the Anglo-Saxons were replaced by new Gallic ones, and in consequence new vocabulary drove out the old. In the space of two or three hundred years English vocabulary was revolutionised by the acquisition of such words.

Obsolete OE words	*Replaced by OF words*
æþeling	prince
ēam	uncle
fulluht	baptism
hǣland	saviour
milts	mercy
rǣdbora	counsellor
sige	victory
stōw	place
wuldor	glory

The radical nature of the change is underlined by the fact that whereas the words *king* and *queen* are English, *advise*, *command*, *commons*, *country*, *court*, *govern*, *parliament*, *peer*, *people*, *Privy Council*, *realm*, *reign*, *royalty*, *rule*, and *sovereign* are all French. As with the terms for government and power, so too with the old concepts for poor and poverty. Thus OE *earm* miserable, *þearfa* destitute, *wǣdl* poverty, and *wǣdla* pauper gave way to *miserable*, *poor*, *destitute*, *poverty*, *pauper*, *mendicant*, etc. And most of the Old English words for war (*gūþ*, *wīg*, *tohte*, etc.) were replaced by *battle*, *conflict*, *strife*, *war*, etc., all of French derivation.

Some Romance words, borrowed at different periods, produced doublets in English:

cadence/chance both ultimately descended from L. cadere 'to fall'
compute/count   computāre
dignity/dainty   dignitās

In most of these the longer form came more or less directly from Latin, and the shorter one from a reduced form produced by phonetic change in France.

Some of these early loan-words show features subsequently

changed or abandoned in the French language itself. English retains, for example, the *s* that the French have abandoned in such words as *beast* and *feast* (*bête* and *fête* in modern French). Similarly the initial *ch-* in many French loan-words came to be pronounced like native words that in Anglo-Saxon were spelt *c-* but pronounced /tʃ/: so *chain*, *charity* (from French, cf. Latin *catēna*, *cāritās*) were Anglicised with initial /tʃ/ to accord with the initial sound of the native words *chaff* (OE *cæf*, *ceaf*), *chalk* (OE *cælc*, *cealc*). In other cases words which had /k/ in Norman French but not in Parisian French came to us in their Norman French form, for example *caitiff* (cf. modF *chétif*), *catch* (cf. modF *chasser*), and *carrion* (cf. modF *charogne*). Anyone considering the nature of the indebtedness of English to French must always keep in mind that most of the loan-words did not come from the central repository of received or standard French but from that variety which happened to be spoken by the Norman conquerors.

From the Conquest until the fourteenth century a French dialect, or 'Anglo-French' as scholars call it, was the accredited language of the Court and of the Law. As a result, many legal terms which came into English from Norman French during this period still remain as part of the central terminology of English law, for example *embezzle*, *judge* (L. *jūdex*, *jūdicem* as noun, *jūdicāre* as verb), *jury*, *larceny*, *lease* (related to modF *laisser* and modE *lax*), *perjury*.

Orthographical changes brought to the language by Norman scribes were very remarkable. The scribes assessed the language they found before them and in general respelt it to accord with their own conventions. They also, in a quite straightforward way, set down the language as it was *used*, without the embellishments and anachronisms employed and preserved by the Anglo-Saxon scribes during the reigns of Edward the Confessor and of Harold.

Among their adventurous innovations was the adoption of the spelling *qu*, especially familiar to them from Latin pronouns, as a replacement for the 'foreign-looking' *cw* of the Anglo-Saxons.

OE	cwealm	→	qualm (modE qualm)
	cwellen	→	quelen (modE quell)
	cwēn	→	queen (modE queen)
	cwic	→	quik (modE quick)

At a stroke this change caused English to take on the outward appearance of a Romance language: *queen* and *quest*, *quick* and *quit*, *quell* and *quiet* were made to look like members of the same linguistic family by the scholarly clerks as they copied their manuscripts.

It is worthy of note that many words of French origin became thoroughly acclimatised as time went on, and in particular those adopted before the middle of the seventeenth century. French words that have come into English since the Restoration have often retained at any rate some of the phonetic or intonational features of the original language. Thus, for example, old borrowings like *baron* (XIII, i.e. thirteenth century), *button* (XIII), and *mutton* (XIII) have fallen into the English dominant pattern, and are always stressed on the first syllable; by contrast the later loan-words *balloon* (XVIII), *bassoon* (XVIII), *cartoon* (XIX), and *platoon* (XVII) are invariably stressed on the second syllable. Similarly *baggage* (XV), *cabbage* (XIV), *homage* (XIII), and *language* (XIII) show the primary accent on the first syllable, and a fully Anglicised /dʒ/ in the unstressed second syllable; whereas *badinage* (XVII), *camouflage* (XX), *entourage* (XIX), and *sabotage* (XX) remain at a kind of half-way house with the main stress on the first syllable but with the last syllable pronounced /ɑːʒ/.

At the end of the Middle English period the English language remained a recognisable branch of the Germanic family, but by the 1470s firmly severed from its western European analogues and not intelligible to them without interpreters. Spoken English continued to diversify but the printers and typesetters, wherever they worked, soon began to set the language down in one spelling system, that of London.

3   EARLY MODERN ENGLISH: 1476 TO 1776

The period 1476 to 1776 was characterised by the establishment of a standard form of written English. It was nevertheless a period of radical change. Writing was no longer restricted to a special few. Pens came into the hands of merchants, artisans, yeomen, and scientists, and they all brought their own linguistic patterns with them, and a preference for the vernacular.

One major feature of the period is that writers of the time took sides and waged battles about Latin neologisms (like *condisciple* fellow-student and *obtestate* to beseech) or 'inkhorn' terms as they came to be called. Writers like Edward Hall and Sir Thomas Elyot were on the side of the new learning, while Sir Thomas More, Sir John Cheke, Thomas Wilson, and others attacked these novelties.

During this period the ceremonial language of Parliament and the Law, and of the Bible and the Book of Common Prayer, settled into a form resembling permanence. It was tinged with Latinity and other elements of antiquity, but was firmly presented in the vernacular. Sheer practical needs also led to the preparation of dictionaries and grammars of English for foreigners seeking refuge in this country from religious oppression in Europe, and then of lexicons and grammatical works for the use of native speakers themselves.

Caxton and the early printers in England broadly accepted the spelling patterns of the late Middle English period and rendered them relatively immobile, though they tolerated more, fairly trivial, variation in detail than is allowed today. For example:

> There was a *damoyselle* that had a pye in a cage.
> This *daymosell* was after moche scorned.

> And it happed that the lord of the *hows* ...
> And in the *hous* therfore was grete sorowe.

The scribes in slightly earlier manuscripts had been much less thorough in the avoidance of casual variation.

Similarly, the spelling of Shakespeare's words in the First Folio (1623) is less rigidly fixed than in modernised systems:

> LEO.   for she was as tender
> As Infancie, and Grace. But yet (*Paulina*)
> *Hermione* was not so much wrinckled, nothing
> So aged as this seemes.
>
>   (*The Winter's Tale*, Act V)

Some of the detailed spelling changes of the period substantially affected the appearance of the language: for example, initial *fn* (ME *fnēsen*, modE *sneeze*) and *wl* (ME *wlatsom* loathsome) disappeared from the language; *gh* or *f* took the place of earlier *h* or *ȝ* (yogh), pronounced /x/ in final position or before another consonant, as in *cough* (ME *coȝe*), *enough* (OE *genōh*), *fight* (OE *feoht*), and *plight* (OE *pliht*). The old runic letter thorn (*þ*) drifted in the way it was written until it so resembled the letter *y* that it had to be abandoned in favour of *th*. Final *s* and *f* after a short vowel passed through periods of great uncertainty (*blis*/*bliss*, *witnes*/*witness*; *bailif*/*bailiff*, *mastif*/*mastiff*) but finally settled down in doubled form. The spelling -*ick* (for earlier -*ic* or -*ik(e)*), as in *academick*, *authentick*, *musick*, *publick*, *stoick*, and so on, adorned the great literary works of the period, and remained as the spelling preferred by Dr Johnson in his *Dictionary* (1755) but not much beyond. The letters *u* and *v*, largely interchangeable or used as mere positional variants in such words as *vnder* (under), *vse* (use), *saue* (save), and *vniuersal* (universal) for much of the period, had divided themselves into their present-day functions by about 1630. So too had *i* and *j* (and *g*): the earlier consonantal use of *i* in words like *ientyl* (gentle), *Iob* (Job), *iudge* (judge), and *reioyce* (rejoice) was abandoned in the early part of the seventeenth century, as was the earlier occasional vocalic use of *j*, as in *jn* (in) and *jngeniously* (ingeniously).

When one turns to vocabulary one cannot but be impressed by the hospitality of the English language. Wave after wave of words entered the language from French, Latin, and Italian, and were for the most part made to conform to the vernacular patterns of spelling and pronunciation. The Renaissance, with its renewed interest in antiquity, also brought a solid vein of Greek words into the language. Smaller clusters of words were adopted from other European countries, especially the Netherlands, and also from much further afield – from Japan, China, and the Dutch East Indies (now Malaysia, Singapore, and Indonesia). Not all the loan-words entered the general language: many of them eked out a temporary existence in literary or scientific works and were then abandoned. Others came to stay and became so thoroughly acclimatised that their original foreignness is no longer evident.

The extent of the French element can be gauged from the following tables, which show the period of first record in each case:

1476–1576	abeyance, colonel, compatible, entertain, grotesque, minion, pioneer, portrait, trophy, vogue
1577–1676	adroit, bayonet, chocolate, fanfare, minuet, moustache, portmanteau, reveille, tube, vehicle
1677–1776	boulevard, brochure, cohesion, envelope, glacier, meringue, précis, salon, vaudeville

In a great many cases it cannot be determined whether a particular word entered English from French or directly from Latin, for example *conclusion* (OF *conclusion*, L. *conclūsiōnem*) and *genitive* (OF *génitif*, fem. *-ive*, L. *genetīvus*).

Italian loan-words of the period include *balcony, ballot, carnival, cupola, lottery, macaroni,* and *squadron*, as well as numerous musical words, for example *cantata, concerto, oratorio,* and *soprano*.

Words from the Netherlands mainly reflect the trade and shipping contacts of the two countries, for example *cruise, freebooter, hawker, keelhaul,* and *yacht*.

Words adopted from more distant countries are usually self-evidently exotic, and many reached English by an indirect route, transmitted through French, Spanish, or medieval Latin. A few examples: *harem, hashish, mufti* (Arabic); *mikado, soy* (Japanese); *kapok, sago* (Malay); *bazaar, shawl* (Persian); and *caviare, kiosk* (Turkish).

Changes in accidence and syntax in the received standard language during the period 1476 to 1776 are important.

The third person present indicative in *-eth* (*he runneth, he liveth*) gave way to *-s* (*he runs, he lives*). In 1476 many nouns had normal plurals in *-(e)n* (*eyen, hosen, housen, shoon,* etc.). By 1776 they had dwindled to the few that still remain in the language: *brethren, children, oxen,* and the archaic *kine*.

The pronominal system developed in various ways. By 1476 the main modern English pronouns (*I, he, she, it, we, us, they,* etc.) existed in the standard language, though some of them were relative newcomers (*she, they, their, them*). *It* lacked a possessive form: *his* (the traditional genitive of (*h*)*it*) or *her* were called on as the context required, as well as such devices as *thereof*:

> Yf salt have loste hyr saltnes what shall be seasoned ther with?
> Vnto the riuer of Egypt and the great sea and the border thereof.

The missing link *its* came into general use in the 1590s.

In 1476 *thou* was the regular form of the singlar second-person pronoun and *ye* the normal plural one. From about 1600 *thou* became reserved for special uses (as in the Bible) and *you* became widely used as the normal form in speech when addressing a single person.

The possessive pronouns *mine, ours, yours,* etc., developed new uses, especially of the type *this house of ours.* The forms *my, our, your,* etc., became gradually restricted to the position immediately before the governed noun (*my book, our children, your grief*).

The most striking changes of all are found in the development of the verbs. The so-called 'strong' verbs – those which changed their stem vowels when used in the past tense, like *ride/rode* (OE *rīdan, rad*) – receded sharply. Many now became established as 'weak': *reap/*pa.t. *rope* (OE *rīpan/rāp*) became *reap/reaped; bow/*pa.t. *beh* (OE *būgan/bēag*) became *bow/bowed.* Others fell out of use altogether or retreated into dialectal use: the Middle English descendants of OE *hrīnan* touch, *snīþan* cut, *stīgan,* ascend, *brēotan* break, and many others. The weak verbs became the dominant class, those which for the most part form their past tense in *-ed.* Nearly all new verbs, whether formed within English or directly adopted from other languages (*contend, elect, fuse, suggest*), were fashioned in the mould of the old 'weak' class. There were a few exceptions, for example *strive* (OF *estriver*), taken over at an earlier date into the native conjugation of *drive,* etc.; and *dig,* originally conjugated weak (*digged*), as always in Shakespeare, the Authorised Version, and Milton, but drawn into the class of strong verbs in the seventeenth century under the influence of verbs like *stick/stuck.* But these were rare.

The third class of older verbs, the irregular or anomalous ones, changed unsystematically as new needs arose, especially the ones traditionally known as 'preterite-present' verbs, the descendants of OE *witan* to know (*wāt* knows, pa.t. *wiste*), *āgan* to own (*āh* owns, pa.t. *āhte*), *cunnan* to know (*cann* know, pa.t. *cūþe*); (without infinitive) *mæg* be able (pa.t. *mihte*), *sceal* be obliged (pa.t. *scolde*), *dearr* dares (pa.t. *dorste*), *mōt* may (pa.t. *mōste*); and also the descendants of the OE verbs *wesan, bēon* to be, *willan* to be willing, *dōn* to do, and *gān* to go.

From this group the language acquired a range of ways of forming the future tense. Wyclif rendered the Latin future tense of verbs in the Bible by *shall* and the present tense of Latin *volo* by *will.* Throughout the period, and in the standard language in Britain to this day, a distinction between *shall* and *will* remained, though it is now fast falling away.

May, might, can, could, ought, and *do* spread their wings and had an extraordinarily complex history between the Old English period and about 1700, by which time most of their present-day functions had been established. For example, *may* started out (in Anglo-Saxon) as a verb of complete predication: OE *ic mæg wel* I am in good health; ME (1398) *Shepe that haue longe taylles may worse* (are less hardy) *wyth wynter than those that haue brode taylles*. It was also a mere, but yet very powerful, auxiliary of predication: *No man may separate me from thee* (1582); *when thou comest there ... thou maist see to the Gate* (Bunyan, 1678). The first use disappeared before 1476. Meanwhile *may* acquired the power to express permission or sanction: *Justice did but (if I may so speak) play and sport together in the businesse* (1653). The intermediate steps, and other uses of *may* before 1776, cannot be briefly described. And so it is with the other auxiliaries.

The old anomalous verbs branched out to enable the language to express periphrastic tenses of commanding usefulness and naturalness to the native speaker, and of equally striking difficulty for foreigners learning the language, expressions of the type *is beaten, is being beaten, will be beaten, has been beaten*; *am eating, will be eating, have been eating*; *will have been shown*; *are you reading?*; *do you believe?*; *I do not believe*, and so on. The virtual absence of such constructions is a striking feature of the language at an earlier stage.

Two other features of the period call for brief mention. As in Old and Middle English, negation continued to be cumulative and not self-cancelling, at least until late in the seventeenth century:

1154   þe erthe ne bar nan corn.
1411   He knoweth wel that ... he ne hath noght born hym as he sholde hav doon.
1568   They should not neede no more to feare him then his shadowe.
1632   Rauenna, which for antiquity will not bow her top to none in Italy.

Finally, the particle *to* followed by an infinitive continued to appear in all the customary circumstances, the so-called 'split' infinitive among them. The construction shades off into antiquity:

c.1400   To enserche sciences, and to perfitly knowe alle manere of Naturels þinges.
1606   To quite rid himselfe out of thraldome.

Just after the secession of the American colonies, Dr Johnson wrote his 'Lives of the Poets', and in the life of Milton he wrote 'Milton was too busy to much miss his wife'.

4   MODERN ENGLISH: 1776 TO THE PRESENT DAY

In 1776 and for some time afterwards the main body of English speakers still lived in the British Isles. English was indisputably a language with its centre of gravity in London. Give or take a few words, George Washington used the same kind of vocabulary as his political equivalent in England. William Cobbett's *Grammar of the English Language*, first published in 1818 in New York, made no formal distinctions between American and British English.

The history of the language during the last two hundred years is one of growth and dissemination on an unprecedented scale. In 1776 there were perhaps 15 million speakers of English, under two million of them in the United States. Now there are estimated to be more than 300 million people whose first language is English, and of these easily the largest number live in the United States. Substantial numbers of English speakers are to be found in Australia, Canada, New Zealand, South Africa, the West Indies, and elsewhere.

Lexical changes in the period from 1776 to the present day are very numerous.

Almost all the normal methods of word formation have been drawn on generously in the modern period. The prefixes *a-*, *de-*, *meta-*, *micro-*, *mini-*, *multi-*, *neo-*, *non-*, *retro-*, and *ultra-* (as well as many others) have been especially prolific, as in *apolitical* (first recorded in 1952), *decaffeinate* (1934), *metastable* (1897), *microcosmic* (1783), *minibus* (1845), *multistorey* (1918), *neo-grammarian* (1885), *non-event* (1962), *retroflexion* (1845), and *ultrasonic* (1923).

Similarly old suffixes like *-ize*, *-less*, *-like*, *-ness*, *-some*, and *-y* have lost none of their formative power, for example *privatize* (1969), *carless* (1927), *pianola-like* (1945), *pushiness* (1920), *chillsome* (1927), and *jazzy* (1919).

Somewhat more complicated formations, though still containing familiar elements, are commonplace, for example *demythologize* (1950), *denazify* (1944), *paraphrasability* (1965), *post-doctoral* (1939) *prepsychotically* (1941), *renormalization* (1948), and *rubbernecker* (1934).

New suffixes of the nineteenth and twentieth centuries include *-burger*, as in *beefburger* (1940) and *cheeseburger* (1938); *-ette*, denoting a female, as in *majorette* (1941), *suffragette* (1909), and *usherette* (1925); *-in*, signifying a large gathering, as in *love-in* (1967), *sit-in* (1937), and *teach-in* (1965); and *-nik* (from Russian or Yiddish), as in *beatnik* (1958), *peacenik* (1965), and *sputnik* (1957).

Back-formations are very numerous, as *reminisce* (verb) (1829) from *reminiscence*, and *window-shop* (verb) from *window-shopping*. So too are shortened or clipped formations like *exam* (1877), *gym* (1871), and *lab* (1895).

Blended words abound, for example *brunch* (breakfast + lunch, 1896), *chortle* (chuckle + snort, 1872), *octopush* (octopus + push, 1970, a kind of underwater hockey), *rurban* (rural + urban, 1918), *savagerous* (savage + dangerous, 1932), Joyce's *scribbledehobble* (scribble + hobbledehoy, 1922), *smaze* (smoke + haze, 1953), and *smog* (smoke + fog, 1903). Closely related are humorous perversions of similarly sounding words, for example *screwmatics* (after *rheumatics*, 1895) and *slimnastics* (after *gymnastics*, 1970).

Rhyming slang has produced a crop of interesting expressions, for example, *apple(s) and pears* (= stairs, 1857), *half-inch* (= to 'pinch', steal, 1925), and *butcher's* (short for *butcher's hook* = look, 1936). Rhyming combinations like *brain-drain* (1963), *fuddy-duddy* (1904), *hanky-panky* (1841), and *walkie-talkie* (1939) continue an old tradition, as do near-rhyming combinations like *ping-pong* (1900).

Newly coined words as such are comparatively rare in the modern period and they tend to look rather unimportant, for example *Oerlikon* (1944), *oomph* (1937), and *oracy* (1965). One of the largest classes of new words at the present time is that which gives us acronyms, that is words formed from the initial letters of (usually) separate words. This technique of word formation seems to be political and military in origin, to judge from the types *Ogpu* (Russ. *Ob"edinënnoe Gosudárstvennoe Politícheskoe Upravlénie*, United State Political Directorate), first recorded in 1923, and *Anzac* (Australian and New Zealand Army Corps), first recorded in 1915. In more recent times they have become very numerous, especially in the period since 1945, and are now admitted to general dictionaries only on a very selective basis. Well-known acronyms include *Nato* (*N*orth *A*tlantic *T*reaty *O*rganisation, set up in 1949) and *radar* (*ra*dio *d*etection *a*nd *r*anging, 1941). But organisations of every kind cast around for a set of initials pronounceable as a word: typical examples of trade union acronyms, for example, are *Aslef* (*A*ssociated *S*ociety of *L*ocomotive *E*ngineers and *F*iremen), COHSE /'kəuzɪ/ (*C*onfederation *o*f *H*ealth *S*ervice *E*mployees), and SOGAT /'səugæt/ (*S*ociety *o*f *G*raphical and *A*llied *T*rades). The great majority of them have no other meaning than the name of the organisation itself, and there are no derivatives. Thus **Aslefer* does not exist in the sense 'a member of Aslef', nor is there a verb *to *aslef*, 'to become a member of Aslef, to act in the manner of members of Aslef', though it seems likely that such derivatives will in due course occur. Many acronyms are so skilfully contrived that they seem to presuppose the existence of genuine Latin, Greek, or Old English words: thus *Nato* has distant echoes of L. *natāre* to swim; *thalidomide* (a near relation of an acronym in that it is formed from ph*thali*mid*o*glutari*mide*) misleadingly suggests some kind of connection with Greek θάλαμος, Latin *thalamus*, an inner chamber; and *rurp* (*r*ealised *u*ltimate *r*eality *p*iton), first recorded in 1968, sounds like an imitative word of native origin (cf. *burp*, *slurp*). Others are made as homonyms of ordinary English words, for example DARE (*D*ictionary of *A*merican *R*egional *E*nglish), *Sarah* (*s*earch *a*nd *r*escue *a*nd *h*oming), the name of a portable radio transmitter, and OWLS, the Oxford Word and Language Service (launched in 1983).

The period since 1776 has witnessed a slowing-down of the rate of absorption of loan-words from foreign languages, though such words are still quite common. By contrast there has been an enormous increase in the outflow of English words to foreign languages – hence the phenomena of *franglais*, Japlish, Spanglish, etc.

The adoption of foreign loan-words is a direct result of culture contact, whether by imperialist conquest, by tourism, or by the receiving of new fashions of food, clothing, entertainment, or the like, in one's own country from abroad. French expressions of varying degrees of naturalisation (*blasé*, *femme de chambre*, *jeune fille*, *pendule*, *porte-cochère*, etc.) abound in nineteenth-century novels. But modern writers tend to look further afield. Travel, war, and politics have brought into our language a great many expressions from all the major languages of the world, many of them awkwardly pronounced and only half understood. A few examples must suffice: from Arabic, *Hadith* (body of traditions relating to Muhammad), *naskhi* (cursive script), *qasida* (elegiac poem), and *rafik* (companion); Chinese, *Lapsang Souchong, mah-jong, Pinyin* (alphabet), *putonghua* (standard spoken language), *qi* (life-force), and loan-translations like *capitalist-roader, running dog,* and *scorched earth*; German, *Bildungsroman, Gestalt, Gestapo, gesundheit* (expression to wish good health), *hausfrau,* and *langlauf* (cross-country skiing); Hebrew, *mazel tov* (good luck!), *Mizpah* (expression of association), *Mizrach* (Judaic practice of turning towards Israel in prayer), *pilpul* (rabbinical argumentation), and *Sabra* (Israeli Jew); Japanese, *happi (coat), Noh, origami* (paper-folding), *pachinko* (kind of pin-ball), and *sashimi* (strips of raw fish); Malay, *langsat* (edible fruit), *merdeka* (freedom), *nasi* (cooked rice), *ronggeng* (popular dance), and *satay* (skewered meat); Russian, *nekulturny* (boorish person), *samizdat, sastruga,* and *sputnik*; and Yiddish, *lox, mazuma, pastrami, schlemiel* (blunderer), and *schmuck* (idiot).

In grammar and syntax the period since 1776 has been characterised, as in earlier periods, by innovation, by new freedoms from traditional constraints, and by numerous other developments. Perhaps the most important development is the incursion of the noun modifier into the traditional territory of the adjective.

From earliest times most adjectives could be used both before the nouns they qualified (OE *strang rāp*, modE *strong rope*) and after, in what is called the predicative position (OE *sē rāp is strang*, modE *the rope is strong*). A few adjectives can be used only in the attributive position (*the utter absurdity of his views*) and some only in the predicative position (*her reply was tantamount to a flat refusal*). But in the last two hundred years, and especially in the twentieth century, there has been a seemingly ungovernable growth in the use of attributive *nouns*, that is of nouns (frequently more than one) used in a position normally occupied by adjectives at an earlier date. A typical example is *Greenham Common peace women*, where the word *women* is preceded by three nouns. It would be possible to construct even longer strings of nouns without wrecking intelligibility. (An account of the rise of noun modifiers is given in my book *The English Language*, pp. 48–50.)

There has also been a substantial increase in the use of the word *one* as what Henry Sweet called a 'prop-word':

> Examples: He rents a house, but I own one.
> Two checked shirts and a blue one.

Important developments by the standards of the eighteenth century have also come about in the way verbs are used, especially in the emergence of new periphrastic forms and in the use of the passive. None of the following constructions could have been used before 1800:

> *We were having a* nice time before you arrived.
> *He is having to* give up smoking.
> *With a view to preventing* waste.
> *He has been known to* be rude to his neighbours.

Another important development in this period has been the virtual demise of the subjunctive mood in modern British English except in formulaic expressions (e.g. *come what may, suffice it to say, be that as it may*) and in an optional use of *were* instead of *was* in expressions like *I wish I were/was dead*.

Despite the remarkable and irreversible changes that have come upon the English language since the Anglo-Saxon period, it has not yet reached a point of perfection and stability such as we sometimes associate with Latin of the Golden Age, the language of Virgil, Horace, and others. Equally it is not entering a period of decline. From earliest times, linguistic radicals have looked at fashionable change and liked it or have not objected to it. Linguistic conservatives have fought to preserve old ways of speaking and writing. The battle continues unabated. The issue is one of sovereignty. Who decides whether it is right to confuse *infer* and *imply, disinterested* and *uninterested*, or *refute* and *deny*? Is *hopefully*, in its new use as a sentence adverb, acceptable, and to whom? Should we all say *kílometre* and condemn *kilómetre*? Is *privatization* to be admitted to the language without dissent?

Battles like these have been fought for centuries. Grievous alterations to the structure of the language, and to individual words, have occurred. These old ambuscades and assaults on the language have been forgotten, but the new ones, here and now, are once more seen by many people as subversive and destructive.

Yet is it not true that our language, far from bleeding to death, still lies ready to hand as a flexible and noble instrument of majesty and strength? The works of modern writers like Virginia Woolf, Iris Murdoch, and T. S. Eliot are as linguistically potent as those of great writers of the past. The oratory of Winston Churchill was not inferior to that of Edmund Burke or Thomas Babington Macaulay. And everyday English, as it is spoken and written by ordinary people, looks like remaining an effective communicative force, though existing in many varieties each of which is subject to perpetual change, for many centuries to come.

Annotated Bibliography

As far as possible, the bibliography lists works of reference that can usually be found in public libraries; and other books that have been published in paperback editions (marked * for paperback; but note that particular titles may have gone into or out of print as paperbacks since this bibliography was compiled). It is arranged as follows:

The English language: General guides; Vocabulary; Grammars; Usage.

Writing English: Guides; 'Style' and copy-editing; Writers and publishing.

THE ENGLISH LANGUAGE

General guides

The Oxford Companion to the English Language, ed. Tom McArthur, Oxford 1992, is a superb A–Z survey of the language in all its strange and wonderful manifestations: English as differently spoken by dozens of nations and communities; English as a lingua franca for the world; English dissected and analysed.

Two well-illustrated encyclopedias by David Crystal also offer a mass of useful information, covering much of the same ground by subjects: *The Cambridge Encyclopedia of Language*, Cambridge 1987*; and, even better, *The Cambridge Encyclopedia of the English Language*, Cambridge 1995. See also I. C. B. Dear, *Oxford English: A Guide to the Language*, Oxford 1986.

Steven Pinker, *The Language Instinct: The New Science of Language and Mind*, London 1994*, argues that language is not a cultural artifact that we learn, but that a language facility is built into the biological make-up of our brains. This is a fascinating book, whether one agrees with the argument or not, and an excellent introduction to linguistics.

Vocabulary

The Oxford English Dictionary, 2nd edn, Oxford 1989 (*OED*) – the great lexicon that is the one indispensable tool for the serious study of the English language – is available not only in libraries in its twenty massive volumes, but also for home use in a single 'compact' volume (new edn, 1991), and on CD-ROM. Of the many good single-volume desk dictionaries of English, two are outstanding: *The Concise Oxford Dictionary of Current English*, 9th edn, Oxford 1995 (*COD*), has definitions of great authority in lapidary form; while *Collins English Dictionary*, 3rd edn, Glasgow 1991 (*Collins*), adds concise encyclopedic entries, biographical, geographical, and historical. For finding elusive words, see Susan M. Lloyd, *Roget's Thesaurus of English Words and Phrases*, Penguin 1984*.

Grammars

Sylvia Chalker and Edmund Weiner, *The Oxford Dictionary of English Grammar*, Oxford 1994, is a modern A–Z approach; Sidney Greenbaum and Randolph Quirk, *A Student's Grammar of the English Language*, Harlow 1990*, is a systematic grammar; both are authoritative, but are not for the faint-hearted.

Usage

The classic text is 'Fowler': H. W. and F. G. Fowler, *A Dictionary of Modern English Usage*, Oxford 1926, splendidly revised in a third edition by R. W. Burchfield, Oxford 1996* (though the first edition is still worth consulting). Also valuable are Eric Partridge, *Usage and Abusage: A Guide to Good English*, rev. edn, London 1965, which, like Fowler, is arranged A–Z; and two guides arranged by subjects, Sir Ernest Gowers, *The Complete Plain Words*, 2nd edn, HMSO 1973 (republished by Penguin, 1973*); and E. S. C. Weiner and Andrew Delahunty, *The Oxford Guide to English Usage*, 2nd edn, Oxford 1993.

WRITING ENGLISH

Guides

There are a number of guides to good English in print which are more elementary than the manuals of usage mentioned above. Here is a selection of them: James Aitchison, *The Cassell Guide to Written English*, London 1994, 1996*; George W. Davidson, *Chambers Good English Guide*, Edinburgh 1985, 1996*; Godfrey Howard, *The Macmillan Good English Handbook*, London 1997; Philip Gooden, *The Guinness Guide to Better English*, Enfield 1996*; and Vivian Summers, *Clear English*, Penguin 1991*.

'Style' and copy-editing

The two most authoritative manuals of 'style' (meaning printer's or publisher's house style, not the author's prose style) are *Hart's Rules for Compositors and Readers at the University Press Oxford*, 39th edn, Oxford 1983; and the *MHRA Style Book: Notes for Authors, Editors, and Writers of Theses*, 5th edn, London 1996*. See also the *Oxford Dictionary for Writers and Editors*, Oxford 1981.

For copy-editing, the standard text is Judith Butcher, *Copy-editing*, 3rd edn, Cambridge 1992.

Writers and publishing

Of the many guides available, Michael Legat, *Writing for Pleasure and Profit*, London 1986*, is sensibly down to earth; as is Barry Turner's *The Writer's Companion*, London 1996*, which takes us ten years further on; Turner includes a useful section on copyright (now in a state of some confusion). For reference, see the annual *Writers' & Artists' Yearbook*.

Libraries will have up-to-date directories of publishing houses. See also Michael Legat, *An Author's Guide to Publishing*, London 1982*.

General Index

The Appendix is not included in the indexes.

Word Index